TOUR GUIDE: INTRODUCTION TO DEBATE

Acknowledgments

This project would not have taken shape without the team of talented folks who contributed to it. Many thanks to Jennifer Courtney, Denise Moore, Chelly Barnard, Leslie Hubbard, Marc Hays, Kathy Donegia, Matt Bianco, Jen Greenholt, Kathi James, Jasmine Flood, Tobin Duby, Jim Parrish, Cyndi Widman, and Anna Willis.

Special thanks to the student-actors who participated in the DVD portions of the debate: Savanna Bradford, Dominic Schell, Terry Dickens, Jr., Carmen Francis, and Leanna Frick.

Classical Conversations, *Tour Guide: Introduction to Debate*

Published by Classical Conversations, Inc.
P.O. Box 909
West End, NC 27376
www.ClassicalConversations.com | www.ClassicalConversationsBooks.com

Cover design by Classical Conversations.

All Scripture quotations, unless otherwise indicated, are taken from the King James Version of the Bible.

Printed in the United States of America.

ISBN 978-0-9972442-0-5

Table of Contents

INTRODUCTION TO Debate

All of us argue, usually badly. As students approach the high school years, it is natural for them to want to forcibly express their opinions. They often do so without thinking through their arguments or pausing to consider the perspective of their audience. Teaching young adults to **debate** properly provides structure for this natural inclination while using impersonal content that allows them to focus on the skill rather than the subject matter of the argument.

Middle school is a good time to begin teaching parts of debate. Students can research current events, make pro and con charts, read papers in front of an audience, and practice eye contact and connecting with the audience while speaking. High school students are ready to learn the simpler competitive forms of debate, and those who enjoy debate can continue to integrate all the aforementioned skills to become effective debaters. Only some people will love debate, but all can benefit from the practice of formal debate, which teaches valuable skills such as:

- Researching for compelling **evidence**
- Separating form from content
- Taking good notes
- Listening actively
- Witholding judgment until an opponent has concluded
- Understanding both sides of an issue
- Constructing logical arguments
- Analyzing logical arguments
- Asking good questions
- Thinking on your feet
- Managing time well
- Speaking from notes AND from scripts
- Practicing formal etiquette
- Disagreeing graciously
- Respecting the ideas of others

Often, debaters are required to argue a position with which they do not agree. Learning all viewpoints helps us form better arguments for our actual beliefs, as it forces us to think beyond inflammatory rhetoric and form cohesive arguments based on the real opinions of those who think differently.

Too often in arguments today, we fail to listen to the other side. We come into an argument determined to beat down the other person with our arguments. This carries the risk that we are

"Debate teaches not only the felicities of speech, but an intellectual courtesy and honesty, as well as a poise and confidence in address that splendidly dramatize the union between the idea and the deed."

—David Hicks, *Norms & Nobility*, 154

DEBATE
: A formal conflict, written or spoken, between competing ideas.

EVIDENCE
: An authority that backs up your argument—includes logical, anecdotal, and empirical information. Team policy debate emphasizes recent empirical evidence while Lincoln-Douglas debate relies more heavily on logic.

not even responding to their actual arguments. Instead, we should come in open to listening carefully to the arguments of another before responding. These skills are very helpful in sharing the gospel. Until a person is heard and loved, it is hard for them to respect a new point of view.

In real life, we are not responsible for the salvation of others; the Holy Spirit is. But we are responsible for pleasing the Lord and boasting in Him before others. We must be ready to give an answer, not to pummel the opponent's intellect with our sharp wit, but to woo them toward The Judge's view and to hear "Well done" from Him. We must also prepare ourselves to recognize false arguments and sentimental persuasion, which lead to wrong conclusions. Debate requires students to recognize logical fallacies in a supportive environment, preparing them for the onslaught of emotional propaganda that pretends to be an argument. Debate helps us to love our neighbor without agreeing with our neighbor.

The point of this small book on debate is to teach beginning debaters the separate forms of team policy and Lincoln-Douglas debates. It does not explain the detailed nuances required to win competitive debates. This book is a companion to a video series that introduces debate through familiar conflicts and characters, teaching students to master the easier parts before they participate in a whole debate. If the structured arguments seem strange to you at first, remember that you learn lots of forms in other subjects: the form of the persuasive essay for writing about literature, the form of the syllogism for formal logic, the form of equations in mathematics, the form of the scientific method, and the form of sentence diagrams in English grammar. Debate is just one more form to master.

Even though the basic forms of debate are easy to learn, debating well is hard work, and parents and instructors should not expect perfection in the first debate or even the first year of debate. Respect for an opponent, listening for both truths and fallacies in an argument, and responding quickly are hard for most of us to do in all forms of dialogue. This requires taking careful notes while listening to something with which you may disagree and withholding your argument until the other person has completely laid out his or her case. These difficult skills are naturally practiced through formal debate and must be practiced repeatedly, but they can only be cultivated after students have mastered a form. This book is intended as a first step toward learning the form of debate. After students have mastered the form, they can choose whether or not to pursue the more difficult skills of competitive debate.

Formal debate belongs to the larger category of persuasive arts. This category includes persuasive essays, Socratic dialogue, and didactic speech. Some persuasive skills are common to all of these forms, but each one also has a specific set of skills appropriate to its form. In formal debate, persuasion depends upon following the rules, which are as important as the content. A great point can be ignored if presented in the wrong form or at the wrong time. This is similar to other structured competitions. For example, you may be able to make a great trick shot from the bleachers with a basketball, but you can't win a basketball game that way. You have to play according to the rules that have been agreed upon by all the interested parties. Debate is a form of community argument with speakers, timers, judges, and an audience discussing principles from antiquity (such as freedom, justice, truth, goodness, and beauty) using evidence and examples from modern times.

AFFIRMATIVE
: The team or speaker whose job is to support the resolution.

NEGATIVE
: The team or speaker whose job is to oppose the resolution.

In team policy debate, students oppose one another in two teams of two people—the **affirmative** team and the **negative** team. The affirmative team tries to persuade the judge that a change in government policy should be made. The negative team defends the current government policy and presents the flaws in the affirmative's argument. Throughout the debate, members of both teams must be able to think on their feet. This is one of the most critical lessons of formal debate. Thinking on your feet as part of a team is very different from being responsible only for your own ideas.

In **Lincoln-Douglas debate**, two individuals face one another instead of two teams of two. Both the affirmative and the negative speaker try to persuade the listeners that a certain **value** is superior to another value. Whereas team policy debate results in action, Lincoln-Douglas debate results in a change in thought.

It is difficult for students to concentrate on form and content at the same time. As we worked on this book and the accompanying videos, we made a conscious choice to use silly examples first so that students could focus on the form. Next, we chose imperfect examples so that students could critique someone else's content before developing their own. If the content were perfect, there would be little to discuss and less to learn.

My hope is that this book will enable new debaters to master the form, experienced debaters to sharpen research and argumentation skills, and intermediate debaters to recognize weak arguments. The book relies on practicing rote presentation, asking good questions, and breaking debate into small components that are easy to practice.

Beginning students are often discouraged by debate forms when the whole form is expected to be learned all at once. The approach presented here is to practice the components in order of difficulty, from the easiest to the hardest. Small steps mastered will free the debater to enjoy the more challenging aspects of debate.

The Spirit of Debate

As devoted sports fans, often gets caught up in the emotion of the outcome of a game. There is nothing wrong with jumping up and down saying, "We won, we won!" and then thanking the referee for doing his best and high-fiving the other team. It becomes wrong when we think the referee has superhuman eyesight and can be belittled for his calls or when we end our victory celebration by greeting the other team with, "Loser..." The players can choose to retaliate for unnecessary roughness or choose to rise above and shake the offender's hand at halftime. We've all seen versions of these actions, and once we are calm, we know what the appropriate course should have been. Friendly competition helps us practice good manners for when the competition in real life isn't friendly.

Competitive debate is about winning, just like football or political elections, and bad behavior can happen in debate just as easily as it can in sports or politics. Students can get flustered, embarrassed, sarcastic, or overbearing. The winning team should laugh and be happy, but then they should remember that there wouldn't have been a win if the other team didn't show up to play. "Winning the race" is a metaphor of God's pleasure in the Bible, but it is not pleasing because you destroyed someone; it is pleasing because you overcame adversity and your own disabilities to accomplish more than you normally expect from yourself.

LINCOLN-DOUGLAS DEBATE
: A one-on-one debate aiming to persuade of a moral claim or judgment.

VALUE
: A moral principle, usually abstract, proposed to govern judgments and decision-making.

A good sport loses graciously, knowing that she also rose above her normal limitations and that all things work to the good of those who love Him. C. S. Lewis reminds us that in heaven as on earth we should be as proud of others' accomplishments as we are of our own because we are a body, and if one member does well, all have done well. Our role in the kingdom that day may have been to encourage another team, not to win. To take a role in administering God's grace is always a blessing, no matter what other rewards we receive.

The debate facilitator can do much to demonstrate to students the parallels between our lives as Christians and the formation of a sustained argument through debate. We do nothing without God's grace, and the opportunity to give grace demonstrates honor. In keeping with this spirit of Christian debate, students should thank the timer and judges often, and judges should remind the students to shake hands when they are finished.

Leigh

Leigh Bortins

INTRODUCTION TO

Team Policy Debate

Team policy debate, or cross-examination debate, has its roots in classical rhetoric. Although the form of debate was not yet established, societies relied on political speech to make decisions in community. The formal structure grew out of debating societies developed in Britain in the 1700s and was refined by American collegiate debating societies from the nineteenth century, which argued topics of public policy much as we do today. These early debates were sometimes based on policy changes, as in the 1897 debate between Wake Forest and Trinity College: "Ought the systems of Water Works, Lighting, and Street Cars be operated by the city for its people, or by private individuals?" What sets policy debate apart is its emphasis on action: choosing a definite course or method of action in response to a problem.

TEAM POLICY DEBATE
A two-on-two debate aiming to change public policy.

The Players' Roles

Judges

In policy debate, the speakers are not trying to persuade each other. Both teams are trying to convince an impartial judge or judges; therefore, students learn to direct their speeches to the judge. This helps the debater argue the **resolution** rather than attacking the person.

During the debate, the judge should take good notes while listening carefully to each speaker. The first responsibility of the judge is not to declare winners and losers; it is to provide feedback that will help both teams improve. The judge should provide verbal or written assessment of research and evidence, lines of argument, questions and answers, persuasiveness, and public speaking skills.

It is not necessary to use a specific competition and judge's form unless you are preparing students to be competitive. The judges' forms are more often used when persons from outside the group need a form of assessment for a competition. We will not address judges' forms in this book since competitive debate is not the main point of this booklet, and since forms vary by organization. Appendix 3 (page 83) contains a sample assessment tool that focuses instead on the skills taught in formal debate.

Our policy debate judges should take the same view as our Father in Heaven. He is pleased with our best as we take the forms He gives us and fill them with appropriate, honoring content. Our assessments should not be used to say, "You were better than he was." Instead, they should inform the students what the judge was persuaded and pleased by and what could be improved.

Any students who are not participating in the debate should practice judging, too, because each day they must weigh the consequences of their own actions, watch out for snares from others, and one day judge principalities with their Brother, our Savior.

Timers

Formal debate is a timed event. Each portion of each debate requires a timer. Use the timer role to introduce a new student to the flow of policy debate or as a specific role if you have an uneven number of students in your debate class. The timer can be a single person or a different person for each side. The timer can be a parent, student, or tutor.

Timing is easy to do and simply requires the timer to pay attention to the sequence of speeches. Each part of a debate has a different amount of time, so a timer quickly learns the order of the

RESOLUTION
: The subject of the debate. In LINCOLN-DOUGLAS, it is the moral proposition; in TEAM POLICY, it is the policy to be changed.

debate. Often the timer acts as facilitator of a debate because her job is to make sure the right person is speaking in the right order for the correct amount of time.

Setting the timer and nodding when ready are the main tasks. It is helpful if the timer can count down for the speaker by raising the appropriate number of fingers to indicate the number of minutes the speaker has left: five at the five-minute mark, four at the four-minute mark, and so on. Use a crooked finger to indicate 30 seconds remaining. It is also helpful if she can put fingers up at 10 seconds left and use fingers to count backwards to the point when she says, "time's up."

Below is a sample schedule so debaters know how much time to prepare for. The times are arbitrary and can be shortened for practice in class. Serious competitors will want to practice speeches for these lengths of time:

1. **Constructive** speeches are 8 minutes
2. **Cross-examinations** are 3 minutes
3. **Rebuttals** are 5 minutes

The timer is also responsible for keeping track of preparation ("prep") time in between speeches. Each team is given a certain amount of **prep time** for the entire debate round, and they treat it like a bank account, withdrawing amounts of prep time before each of their speeches. For example, your class or debate club may give a total of five minutes of prep time per team. If a speaker wants two minutes to prepare, he must inform the timer, who keeps track of all the prep minutes and tells the team when their prep time has been exhausted.

CONSTRUCTIVE
: A longer speech that sets the parameters for the debate, building arguments and reinforcing them against the other side's attacks.

CROSS-EXAMINATION
: A short, formal question-and-answer session after each CONSTRUCTIVE speech designed to clarify arguments and expose weaknesses.

REBUTTAL
: A shorter speech that summarizes the arguments made in the CONSTRUCTIVES and argues for the superiority of the speaker's side.

PREP TIME
: Time allotted to each speaker or team for the entire debate, to be parceled out before their speeches.

STATUS QUO
: The current system or policy that the affirmative wants to change.

Coaches and Facilitators

The debate facilitator and the judge are often the same person. A coach or facilitator does not need to be an expert to begin coaching debate. This resource, as well as hundreds online, can help the coach improve right along with the students. New coaches need to be given the same grace to fail as new students. Formal debate is not a cultural norm, and the only way to reinvigorate it as an art is to jump right in and try.

The only qualification needed is the willingness to learn debate and to help the debaters learn one step at a time. This guide is designed just for you.

A Quick Checklist of Things to Teach Debaters

1. Introduce yourself and conclude with a reminder of the resolution.
2. Think of problems society needs to solve.
3. Research who currently tries to solve them and how.
4. Think through the benefits of the **status quo** versus policy changes.
5. Stand in front of an audience while making eye contact.
6. Find more advanced debate material if you are enjoying debate.

In debate clubs and classes, it can be good to alternate between pairing unequally skilled debaters (so one can train the other) and pairing equally skilled debaters (so both can experience success beyond their individual capabilities). For actual debates, try to pair equally skilled teams so both teams can experience some success.

A debate facilitator ideally has four students, or two teams with two students each. A debate can take two hours to complete if you keep to competition times. This can make it difficult for a facilitator with more students or an uneven number. Below are some suggestions for handling uneven numbers or time constraints:

1. The coach can fill in at practice.
2. One debater can have a week off and be the timer and judge.
3. Instead of a two-versus-two debate, have a one-on-one policy debate for instructional purposes and to keep all the students engaged. This option is not as effective since the script is for two versus two, but the debaters can at least research, present a case, and cross-examine each other.
4. Create teams of three so that a new debater can apprentice with a team that has more experience.
5. Shorten each speech time by a minute or more.

The form of policy debate provides enough boxes to check off. Be flexible with humans.

Debaters

Team policy typically has four roles for debaters, divided into two teams. The affirmative team consists of the 1A (the first affirmative) and the 2A (the second affirmative). The negative team consists of the 1N (the first negative) and the 2N (the second negative). Each speaker gets to present two speeches, listen to the other team's speeches, and ask and answer cross-examination questions. Later, we'll talk about the different responsibilities of each of these four speakers.

The basic philosophy of the affirmative team is that change needs to happen. The affirmative team is optimistic that change will bring improvement, and the benefits outweigh the potential risks. The negative team, by contrast, would rather preserve the status quo (the current state of affairs). They argue that change is not necessary and comes with greater risks than rewards.

The Resolution

Though not a player, the resolution is the driving force of a debate. It sets the topic for debate and tells the affirmative team what to propose and the negative team what to reject. The resolution always takes a specific form and is addressed in specific ways:

> "Resolved: This policy should be changed."

Examples include,

1. Resolved: The death penalty should be abolished.
2. Resolved: The United States should reform its policy toward its territories.
3. Resolved: The United States should significantly change its immigration policy.
4. Resolved: The United States' election laws should be substantially revised.

The resolutions should clearly state the debate's topic but be broad enough to encourage research and strategy. The debaters must stay on-topic or they will automatically lose the debate. For example, if you are arguing for mandatory health insurance, be sure not to argue for mandatory health care, as they are not the same thing. One of the first things debaters must do is define the terms used in the resolution.

The affirmative team affirms or agrees with the resolution. They say things like, "We urge the judges to vote FOR the resolution." The negative team negates or disagrees with resolution. They say things like, "We urge the judges to vote AGAINST the resolution."

New debaters often think two things are being discussed and try to change the resolution. For example, if the resolution is "Taxes must be decreased," they try to change the negative position to "Taxes must be increased." This is the wrong approach.

The affirmative team is FOR "Taxes must be decreased" and the negative team is AGAINST "Taxes must be decreased." The resolution is the same for both sides. The teams just differ in whether they are FOR or AGAINST the same resolution.

THE BASICS OF TEAM POLICY DEBATE

The Debater's Role While Speaking

Team policy debate is an orderly argument among two teams of two people. It is similar to a play with a script. The script in Appendix 4 is a silly example of a full team policy debate. Debate classes can read the script aloud together to give the debaters a general idea of what they are about to learn.

This next section will examine what happens in each part of the debate, so you may want to read the sample script before continuing. We'll begin in a casual manner and eventually proceed to more correct use of words and dialogue. You may notice that we introduce formal debate terms like "resolution," "harms," and "advantages" conversationally rather than didactically at first: don't worry—we will go back and define those terms in detail later on.

FIRST AFFIRMATIVE CONSTRUCTIVE

A person who wants to make a case for a policy change:

1. Introduces himself.
2. Defines some terms.
3. Explains a problem with a certain public policy. (harms)
4. Offers a **solution**.
5. Explains why it is a good solution.
6. Concludes by asking the audience to affirm this solution.

In a debate, this speech is called the First Affirmative Constructive (1AC) because the presenter is the first one to speak, affirms (agrees) with the need for change, and constructs an argument for the change in policy. This speech is called a "constructive" because it constructs (builds) the foundations of the argument in favor of the resolution.

CROSS-EXAMINATION

Two people who don't want to make the change have been listening and thinking about what the first person (1A) has just shared. They are called the negative team. They do not agree that the case should be affirmed; they believe it should be voted against, or negated.

Now they get a chance to ask the affirmative speaker some questions, called cross-examination. The questioner asks for clarification on the points made by the first person. It would be silly to argue against a case that you don't understand, so these questions tend to be very basic. This questioner should also ask for a copy of the affirmative's case so his partner can be preparing arguments while listening.

SOLUTION
: Another name for the PLAN.

PLAN
: A change in policy designed to fix the HARMS.

1. May I have a copy of your case?
2. Can you please repeat your first point?
3. What was the source of your evidence?
4. Did you explain how you are going to pay for your **plan**?

While the negative speaker is asking these questions, his teammate is listening and preparing to address the first person's case. This teammate's job to explain that the status quo (which means the current policy) is just fine and that the first person is wrong about a need for a policy change.

In summary, a person called the First Affirmative has introduced a policy change. The next person, part of the negative team, has asked clarifying questions to be sure he and his teammate really understand the First Affirmative's arguments for change. His teammate, who is called the First Negative, is now about to stand up and argue against the First Affirmative's case.

FIRST NEGATIVE CONSTRUCTIVE CASE

This speech is called the First Negative Constructive (1NC) because it constructs (builds) the foundations of the argument in opposition to the resolution. Unlike the First Affirmative speaker, this debater doesn't have the benefit of a pre-written argument. Instead, the First Negative must argue against each point in the First Affirmative's case. If she doesn't address a point, the audience assumes that the negative either agrees with the point or thinks it is too insignificant to give any attention and so they concede that point to the affirmative's case.

So the person who does not want to make a change:

1. Introduces herself.
2. Explains if she thinks a term should be defined differently.
3. Explains why there is no problem with a certain public policy.
4. Demonstrates why the affirmative's solution is in error.
5. Explains why the change does not have the benefits shared by the affirmative.
6. Concludes by asking the audience, a judge, NOT to affirm the change.

CROSS-EXAMINATION

The person who began the whole debate, the First Affirmative, now gets to question the First Negative.

After all, the affirmative speaker thinks he just laid out a wonderful new change and wants to understand why his esteemed colleagues don't think it is so wonderful. This is his time to not only clear up misunderstandings with the negative team but also to ask questions to help the audience see problems with the current policy.

In this cross-examination, the First Affirmative asks questions of the First Negative. Everyone else is listening.

1. What was the source of your evidence?

2. Did you mention the first problem we pointed out?
3. Could you please repeat your second argument against our plan?

In summary, the First Affirmative introduced an argument for change. The negative team cross-examined the First Affirmative for clarity on the argument. Then the First Negative explained why the change is not needed. Then the First Affirmative asked the First Negative questions to demonstrate the strength of the affirmative case.

Now, the affirmative team has a second member who has been listening and taking notes. This teammate has had time to think through all the attacks on the affirmative case and is now ready to defend her partner.

SECOND AFFIRMATIVE CONSTRUCTIVE

The First Affirmative's teammate is called the Second Affirmative. She must outline the exact same points as the First Affirmative; otherwise, the audience will think that the affirmative team has now recognized a weak point in their case and doesn't want to bring it up again. This would demonstrate that they have conceded a point to the negative team. In real life, you might realize you have a weakness in an argument and drop it when someone points out that it is not an effective argument. This is where formal debate is different from real life. The Second Affirmative must address the weak point, but may not spend much time on it, choosing to amplify all the better arguments originally made.

The second person who wants to make a change:

1. Introduces herself.
2. Points out why her **definitions** are superior.
3. Reiterates the problem with a certain public policy, using new evidence.
4. Clarifies her solution.
5. Verifies that it is a good solution, despite what the other person argued.
6. Concludes by asking the judges to affirm the need for change, technically called a resolution.

CROSS-EXAMINATION

Now the First Negative gets to cross-examine the affirmative speaker. By now everyone should understand the main parts of the argument. It's time to question the details of the affirmative's case and ask questions like:

1. Where did you get your information; is it timely?
2. Do you have proof that your solution works?
3. Is your evidence biased or reliable?

SECOND NEGATIVE CONSTRUCTIVE CASE

The first person to ask questions or cross-examine was from the negative team. Now he gets to add to the case against the affirmative. This is the second constructive speech that the negative

DEFINITION
The meaning of key terms in the RESOLUTION, proposed by the affirmative to set the boundaries of the debate.

team has given, so it is called the Second Negative Constructive (2NC). Every debater gets a chance to construct a case and cross-examine an opponent. The swapping of roles makes debating difficult at first because no one is sure who goes next and what they are doing. The next chapter will address ways to practice the sequence of the debate.

The Second Negative has heard the affirmative case from two people and he has asked some clarifying questions. He listened to his teammate, the First Negative, make an attempt to counter the case in general, then he heard the affirmative cross-examiner point out weaknesses in the First Negative's points. The Second Negative should have some real ammunition. Again, he must keep to the points introduced by the First Affirmative. In real-life arguments, people's thoughts go astray and they end up arguing about different things than they started with. Sloppy thoughts are discouraged in debate. Keep to the arguments already presented or it will look like you don't know how to listen or don't understand the policy.

So the Second Negative stands and:

1. Introduces himself.
2. Explains why there really isn't a problem, despite what the last speaker said.
3. Explains why there is no need for the affirmative solution.
4. Explains how the solution proposed doesn't really fix the problems and will cause other problems.
5. Concludes by asking the judge NOT to vote for the resolution.

Cross-Examination

Now the Second Affirmative gets her chance to be the cross-examiner. This is the last time anyone is allowed to ask questions, so they should be very thoughtful.

1. If this problem exists, would you agree that it's a big deal?
2. Did you address the second problem we brought up?
3. Did you give evidence that our solution will cause other problems?

FIRST NEGATIVE REBUTTAL

DISADVANTAGES
: A negative outcome or consequence resulting from the affirmative PLAN.

NEGATIVE BLOCK
: Two back-to-back negative speeches comprising the last constructive speech and the first rebuttal.

HARM
: A problem that exists because of the current policy.

Everyone takes a breath and a few minutes to meet with their partners because things are about to change. Instead of the affirmative team getting the next speech, the negative team will get to speak again. This is what is called the **Negative Block**. All points in the case should continue to be addressed, but the form is a little looser.

The First Negative stands up and reintroduces herself. Remember, there are four people going back and forth, and you want the judge to be clear on who is who. The First Negative ties together everything that has been said in a way that will help the judge see that the affirmative team has not made a strong enough case to change public policy.

Now that cross-examinations are done, neither team has a chance to ask clarifying questions, so the rule is "no new arguments in the rebuttals." Both teams have had a chance to establish their positions, and now they must stop building and start defending.

1. The affirmative laid out these problems, or **harms**, but their data was old or insufficient.

2. The affirmative laid out this solution, but it costs too much, or there is no one to enforce it.
3. The affirmative says their solution will give us benefits, but really it will create new problems.
4. Therefore, I urge the judges to vote AGAINST the resolution.

FIRST AFFIRMATIVE REBUTTAL

Now the First Affirmative stands up and reintroduces himself. He gives more examples and support for his case without changing any of the arguments. It is important not to bring up new arguments in the rebuttals because, with no more cross-examinations left, the other team does not have a chance to ask clarifying questions about new arguments.

1. The affirmative has another resource that backs up the data about the harms, proving its accuracy and confirming the sources' credentials.
2. The affirmative disagrees with the negative's analysis of the cost because the negative team forgot to think about a hidden cost of the status quo.
3. The affirmative verifies their solution works because another state or country is doing the same thing successfully. There will be no adverse effects.
4. Therefore, I urge the judges to vote FOR the resolution.

SECOND NEGATIVE REBUTTAL

Now the Second Negative stands up and reintroduces himself. He must be as persuasive as possible, as this is the last time we will hear from the negative team.

1. The affirmative does have compelling data for the harms (the point that the affirmative was strongest in) but only if you agree with their wrong presuppositions and ignore the bias of their evidence.
2. The affirmative's solution does nothing to improve life for our citizens as evidenced by our data on current policy.
3. The negative has pointed out repeatedly (the negative's strong point) that the improvements the affirmative has brought out only support a special interest group and are not for the benefit of the general public. Instead of benefits, the plan will cause more problems.
4. Therefore, I urge the judges to vote AGAINST the resolution.

SECOND AFFIRMATIVE REBUTTAL

Now it is the last speaker's turn. Because the affirmative team has the **burden of proof** and must defend every part of their case, they get the last word in the debate round. It has been a heated debate, but everyone followed the sequence of arguments. The First Affirmative came in believing he had a good idea and that it was worth getting his fellow policy makers to consider his points. The Second Affirmative sees some weaknesses, but the policy can be slightly modified when she gets it on paper if this committee will just affirm that is a policy our citizens will endorse. She's thankful that her teammate was present to think about the negative's arguments

BURDEN OF PROOF
The affirmative's obligation to substantiate claims, where the negative may simply cast doubt.

and take notes so that in the end the policy will be supported by not just her colleagues but all of their constituents. Her teammate's questions really helped the judge see that the negative's short-term pragmatism cannot be allowed to trump long-term benefits for all citizens. And she is grateful that her opponents pushed back and helped her see how to strengthen her arguments. Here goes!

1. There are some serious problems harming our country, proven by evidence from valid sources with strong credentials. I think we can solve these problems with this policy change.
2. The changes mandated by this solution will use current funds, a current department to administrate it, and a current agency to enforce it. So there are no new costs to the taxpayers.
3. The negative has spent a fair amount of time trying to make the point that the **advantages** of our new policy are all smoke and mirrors, but we have proved our advantages with multiple pieces of evidence, while the negative has only asked questions and made assertions.
4. Therefore, my partner and I urge the judges to vote FOR the resolution.

Now let's take the big ideas that we've just covered and look at them in outline form, using the terminology of team policy debate.

ADVANTAGE(S)

A positive outcome, typically reversing a HARM, resulting from the affirmative PLAN.

The Debater's Role While Speaking: Double Time!

As we've just seen, every debater gets to construct a case, cross-examine an opponent, take notes, prepare, and give a rebuttal. The process of just standing to present at the proper time is important to practice.

Using this outline, have all four debaters walk through their roles until they can do so without looking at the outline. This is very important to practice so the debaters can do so without thinking. They have enough to think about.

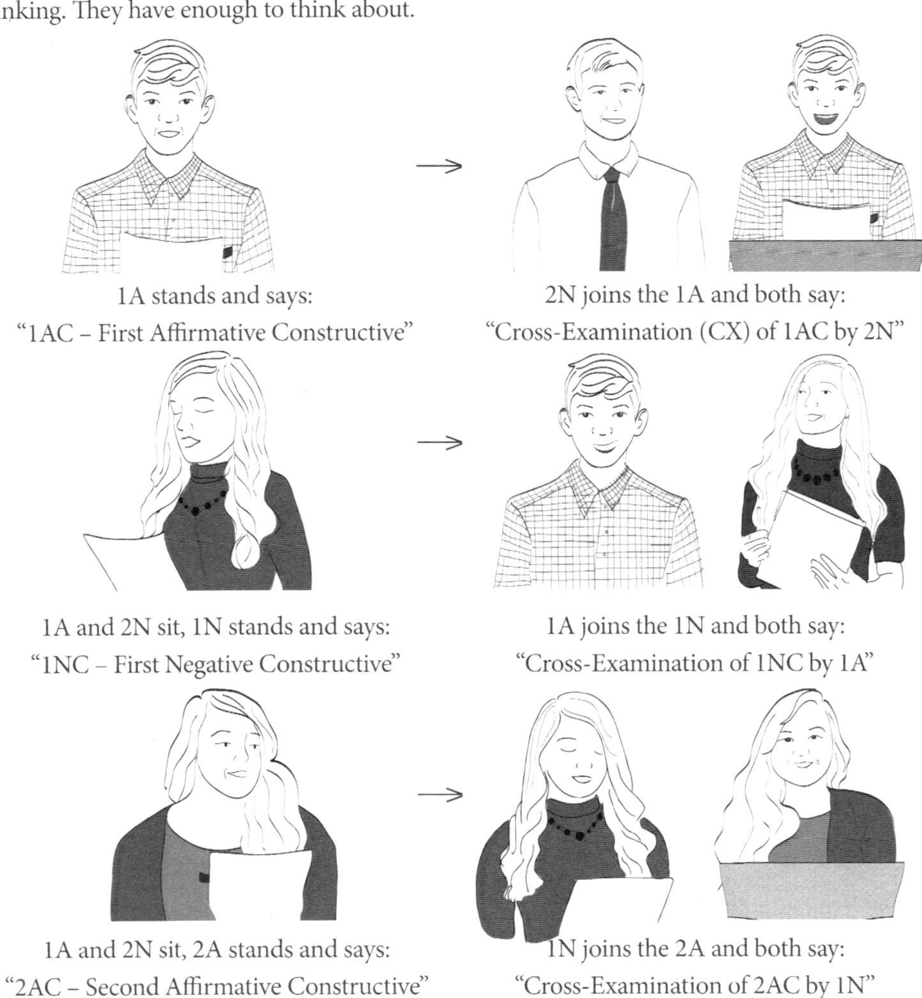

1A stands and says:
"1AC – First Affirmative Constructive"

2N joins the 1A and both say:
"Cross-Examination (CX) of 1AC by 2N"

1A and 2N sit, 1N stands and says:
"1NC – First Negative Constructive"

1A joins the 1N and both say:
"Cross-Examination of 1NC by 1A"

1A and 2N sit, 2A stands and says:
"2AC – Second Affirmative Constructive"

1N joins the 2A and both say:
"Cross-Examination of 2AC by 1N"

1N and 2A sit, 2N stands and says:
"2NC – Second Negative Constructive"

2A joins the 2N and both say:
"Cross-Examination of 2NC by 2A"

2A and 2N sit, 1N stands and says:
"1NR – First Negative Rebuttal"

1N sits, 1A stands and says:
"1AR — First Affirmative Rebuttal"

1A sits, 2N stands and says:
"2NR – Second Negative Rebuttal"

2N sits, 2A stands and says:
"2AR — Second Affirmative Rebuttal"

Notice that the First Affirmative speaks first throughout. He has the first constructive speech, gets the first chance to cross-examine the negative team, and gives the first rebuttal. The Second Affirmative speaks second throughout. She has the second constructive speech, gets the second chance to cross-examine the negative team, and gives the second rebuttal.

The negative team follows this pattern with their speeches, but they cross-examine in the opposite order: the Second Negative does the first cross-examination since his partner is preparing to give the 1NC.

Also notice the negative block (the two back-to-back negative speeches comprised of the 2NC and the 1NR), which serves two purposes: it gives the negative team an advantage to make up for the fact that the affirmative has the first and the last word, and it also makes it possible for the affirmative team to speak first and last.

This outline is similar to the outline of a mock trial, in which the prosecution speaks first and last because they have the burden of proof, just as the affirmative team does here. The prosecution must prove that the defendant is guilty beyond a reasonable doubt. Similarly, the affirmative team in a debate has the burden of proving that there is a need for a new plan. In contrast, the defense simply has to open the door for doubt. Likewise, the negative team in debate must simply create doubt that a change is needed.

The Affirmative Constructive in Team Policy Debate

Because the affirmative team, as the team proposing a change, has the burden of proof, the First Affirmative Constructive speech becomes the blueprint for the rest of the debate. It is the only speech in team policy debate that is scripted ahead of time—all of the other speeches derive from this one—so if debaters can master this form, they will be more than halfway to their goal.

It is easiest to learn a new concept by doing things in small, additive portions. Like practicing scales of music or dribbling a basketball, rote practice is required to internalize the mechanics of debate. Master the easy things first and then spend time on the parts that take a lifetime to master.

Learn the form, and then concentrate on using the form while listening and thinking at the same time. Students can use the following example as a template when writing their own First Affirmative Constructive speeches.

INTRODUCTION, RESOLUTION, AND CONCLUSION

Every debater should stand in front of the room and read:

> Good morning. My partner, [partner's name], and I, [your name], are FOR the resolution: "Taxes should be increased."
>
> ...
>
> In conclusion: "Taxes should be increased."
>
> Therefore, my partner, [partner's name], and I, [your name], urge the judges to vote FOR the resolution.
>
> Thank you. I am now ready for cross-examination.

You have now used the form to open and close a team policy debate.

Now every debater should stand in front of the room and say the same thing without reading or notes. Say it from memory.

Next, every debater should stand in front of the room and say the same thing without reading or notes. Say it from memory, but change one word. Instead of FOR say AGAINST the resolution.

DEFINITIONS

Definitions can seem like a waste of time until you realize most arguments are over definitions.

Is abortion murder? Is war murder? Is accidental killing murder? Is self-defense murder? People who care about ideas also care about the words used to express the ideas and work to provide clarity.

Every debater should stand in front of the room and read:

Good morning. My partner, [partner's name], and I, [your name], are FOR the resolution: "Taxes should be increased."

Observation I: Definitions

Taxes: money collected from citizens to pay for government services

Should be: state of affirmation

Increased: added to, made more of

...

In conclusion: "Taxes should be increased."

Therefore, my partner, [partner's name], and I, [your name], urge the judges to vote FOR the resolution.

Thank you. I am now ready for cross-examination.

Let's ask questions about what we just said.

- Why do we have to list sources for definitions?
- Are they legitimate sources?
- What makes a resource legitimate?

HARMS

Every debater should stand in front of the room again and read:

Good morning. My partner, [partner's name], and I, [your name], are FOR the resolution: "Taxes should be increased."

Observation I : Definitions

Taxes: money collected from citizens to pay for government services
Source: *Democracy for Everyone* by Tom Jenkins

Should Be: state of affirmation
Source: *Webster's Dictionary*, 2011

Increased: added to, made more of
Source: *Webster's Dictionary*, 2011

Observation 2: Harms

Harm 1: Schools are underfunded.
Source: *New York Times*

Harm 2: The poor need more health care.
Source: *Wall Street Journal*

...

In conclusion: "Taxes should be increased."

Therefore, my partner, [partner's name], and I, [your name], urge the judges to vote FOR the resolution.

Thank you. I am now ready for cross-examination.

OBSERVATION
One of the pillars of a formal debate.

Let's evaluate what we just said:

- Why do we have to list harms?
- Do we need a policy change if nothing is wrong?
- Are the resources reliable for this kind of information?
- Did you remember to say "Observation II" and "Point A" and "Source" aloud?
- Does it help your audience follow your argument if you have a clearly stated outline?

Debates are timed and you want to use that time effectively. Debaters use consistent words as indicators to abbreviate phrases. Instead of wasting time saying, "I got my information from...", they just say "Source." Once we have read the whole constructive speech aloud, the outline and indicating words will be obvious.

SOLUTION (PLAN)

Every debater should stand in front of the room again and read:

Good morning. My partner, [partner's name], and I, [your name], are FOR the resolution: "Taxes should be increased."

Observation I: Definitions

Taxes: money collected from citizens to pay for government services
Source: *Democracy for Everyone* by Tom Jenkins

Should Be: state of affirmation
Source: *Webster's Dictionary*, 2011

Increased: added to, made more of
Source: *Webster's Dictionary*, 2011

Observation 2: Harms

Harm 1: Schools are underfunded.
Source: *New York Times*

Harm 2: The poor need more health care.
Source: *Wall Street Journal*

Observation 3: Plan

Mandates: Increase income taxes by 3% on people with incomes over $200,000

Agency: Internal Revenue Service

Funding: Normal means

Enforcement: Internal Revenue Service

...

In conclusion: "Taxes should be increased."

Therefore, my partner, [partner's name], and I, [your name], urge the judges to vote FOR the resolution.

Thank you. I am now ready for cross-examination.

MANDATE
The specific law(s) or policy change(s) your plan is proposing.

AGENCY
The branch of goveernment or department that will pass your plan.

FUNDING
The means you will use to pay for your plan.

ENFORCEMENT
The people responsible for enforcing your plan.

Let's evaluate what we just said.

- Why do policy changes need funding?
- What kind of plans need enforcement?
- Did you remember to say "Mandates," "Agency," "Funding," and "Enforcement" aloud?

ADVANTAGES

Every debater should stand in front of the room again and read:

Good morning. My partner, [partner's name], and I, [your name], are FOR the resolution: "Taxes should be increased."

Observation I: Definitions

Taxes: money collected from citizens to pay for government services
Source: *Democracy for Everyone* by Tom Jenkins

Should Be: state of affirmation
Source: Webster's Dictionary, 2011

Increased: added to, made more of
Source: *Webster's Dictionary*, 2011

Observation 2: Harms

Harm 1: Schools are underfunded.
Source: *New York Times*

Harm 2: The poor need more health care.
Source: *Wall Street Journal*

Observation 3: Plan

Mandates: Increase income taxes by 3% on people with incomes over $200,000

Agency: Internal Revenue Service

Funding: Normal means

Enforcement: Internal Revenue Service

Observation 4: Advantages

Advantage 1: Schools will have more resources.
Source: *The Washington Post*

Advantage 2: More people will be healthier.
Source: *Christian Science Monitor*

In conclusion: "Taxes should be increased."

Therefore, my partner, [partner's name], and I, [your name], urge the judges to vote FOR the resolution.

Thank you. I am now ready for cross-examination.

Let's evaluate what we just said.

- Did you notice that the advantages are a reflection of the harms?
- Why would it be a problem to have three harms and only two advantages?
- Do the advantages follow from the solution?
- How could you attack the advantages?
- Is there a better way to achieve these advantages? A less expensive way?

The harms, solution, and advantages are a package. They must all be intertwined, or else this policy is probably not a good fix.

Congratulations! At this point you have read an entire First Affirmative Constructive case and asked good cross-examination questions. Now you have the framework to start thinking about debate from the negative perspective.

The Negative Constructive in Team Policy Debate

Even though the Second Affirmative Constructive is unscripted, too, this speaker can usually mimic the form of the First Affirmative Constructive, simply adding evidence and answering the negative team's attacks. By contrast, the negative team often feels lost at first, as neither speaker gets to begin with a pre-written case. Advanced and competitive debaters are trained to construct a case against the affirmative's arguments on the fly. They are able to do this because they have researched a single topic for a long time and have seen and participated in many debates. For beginning debaters, that task can be daunting! So how do we train debaters to acquire this skill without scaring them away?

If you're coaching beginning debaters, one option is to choose a resolution that only has two possible sides such as "The death penalty should be abolished" or "The voting age should be lowered." Then the negative team can essentially construct a case against the resolution rather than needing to anticipate the affirmative team's arguments.

To construct a case against the resolution, the negative team should:

1. Meet to determine who will research which topics and how to organize the research to share.
2. Write the outline of the negative argument that both partners will use.
3. Gather enough evidence to provide additional support for your case.
4. Insert key supporting evidence into speech using the same outline as the affirmative case.
5. During the round, listen enough to respond to cross-examination questions.

As students become more comfortable with the form, you can tackle a more complex resolution with multiple possibilities for affirmative cases such as "The United States should significantly change its immigration policy" or "The United States should reform its policy toward the Middle East." Then, the negative team's job will be more difficult, but they can still prepare ahead of time, using these strategies:

1. Meet to determine who will research which topics and how to organize the research to share.
2. Research the policy itself: what it is, how it works, who it benefits, and who it hurts.
3. Research the things that are good about the current policy.
4. Make a list of possible policy changes (what the affirmative may say); then research 2–3 weaknesses of each one.
5. Gather some basic information about funding and enforcement—for example, "Our national debt is too high, so we shouldn't take on new costs," or "Our federal agencies are overworked, so we shouldn't increase their workload."
6. During the round, ask a lot of questions. Remember, the affirmative has the burden of proof.

✢ Preparation is the first step to becoming a successful negative team.

Let's look at a sample Negative Constructive in outline form, distinguishing what is prepared ahead of time from what is added during prep time. The "E" indicates evidence (a quotation or statistic).

	Notes from 1AC	Neg prepared before debate	Neg added during debate
Resolution	Taxes should be increased.	Taxes should not be increased.	
Definitions	Taxes: money from citizens to pay for gov. services. Should be: affirmation Increased: added to	[Negative prepares own definitions, ready to propose if needed.]	
Harms	1. Schools underfunded. 2. Poor lack health care.	Lack of taxes is not the problem; misuse of resources is.	**(E)** Schools pay ++ $$$ per student. Isn't working.
Plan	Mandates: +3% income tax if >$200,000 Agency: IRS Funding: X Enforcement: IRS		These people are job creators. We're hindering their ability. With higher taxes, will need more enforcement. That costs $$. None provided.
Advantages	1. + Resources for schools. 2. Healthier people	Throwing money at problems doesn't fix them. **(E)** Adding taxes will hurt people more than it helps.	**(E)** Schools fundamentally broken. Can't fix with $$.

The negative team would have gathered evidence to attack potential harms, plans, and advantages, and even though they might not use all of it, they have it ready to go. Students can use the following example as a template when preparing to give their own negative constructive speeches.

INTRODUCTION, RESOLUTION, AND CONCLUSION

Every debater should stand in front of the room and read:

> Are the judges ready? Is the timer ready?
>
> Good morning. My name is [your name], and my partner, [partner's name], and I stand AGAINST the resolution: "Taxes should be increased."
>
> ...

In conclusion, I urge the judges to REJECT the resolution, "Taxes should be increased." Thank you. I am now ready for cross-examination.

Now every debater should stand in front of the room and say the same thing without reading or notes. Say it from memory.

DEFINITIONS

Every debater should stand in front of the room and read:

> Are the judges ready? Is the timer ready?
>
> Good morning. My name is [your name], and my partner, [partner's name], and I stand AGAINST the resolution: "Taxes should be increased."
>
> **Observation 1: Definitions**
>
> The negative accepts the affirmative's definitions.
>
> ...
>
> In conclusion, I urge the judges to reject the resolution, "Taxes should be increased." Thank you. I am now ready for cross-examination.

HARMS

Every debater should stand in front of the room and read:

> Are the judges ready? Is the timer ready?
>
> Good morning. My name is [your name], and my partner [partner's name] and I stand AGAINST the resolution: "Taxes should be increased."
>
> **Observation 1: Definitions**
>
> The negative accepts the affirmative's definitions.
>
> **Observation 2: Harms**
>
> Harm 1: The affirmative team said that schools are underfunded, BUT schools pay a lot of money per student and still fail.
>
> > QUOTE: "The public schools in Washington, DC spent $29,349 per pupil in the 2010–2011 school year, according to the latest data from National Center for Education Statistics, but in 2013, fully 83 percent of the eighth graders in these schools were not 'proficient' in reading and 81 percent were not 'proficient' in math." END QUOTE
> >
> > SOURCE: Terence P. Jeffrey, CNSNews.com, May 14, 2014.
> >
> > SUMMARY: A lack of money is not the issue—poorly used resources is.
>
> Harm 2: The affirmative team said that poor people need more health care, BUT, again, a lack of money is not the issue—poorly used resources are.
>
> ...
>
> In conclusion, I urge the judges to REJECT the resolution, "Taxes should be increased." Thank you. I am now ready for cross-examination.

SUMMARY
: A brief explanation in your own words of how your evidence proves your point.

PLAN

Every debater should stand in front of the room and read:

Are the judges ready? Is the timer ready?

Good morning. My name is [your name], and my partner, [partner's name], and I stand AGAINST the resolution: "Taxes should be increased."

Observation 1: Definitions

The negative accepts the affirmative's definitions.

Observation 2: Harms

Harm 1: The affirmative team said that schools are underfunded, BUT schools pay a lot of money per student and still fail.

QUOTE: "The public schools in Washington, DC spent $29,349 per pupil in the 2010–2011 school year, according to the latest data from National Center for Education Statistics, but in 2013, fully 83 percent of the eighth graders in these schools were not 'proficient' in reading and 81 percent were not 'proficient' in math." END QUOTE

SOURCE: Terence P. Jeffrey, CNSNews.com, May 14, 2014.

SUMMARY: A lack of money is not the issue—poorly used resources is.

Harm 2: The affirmative team said that poor people need more healthcare, BUT, again, a lack of money is not the issue: poorly used resources is.

Observation 3: Plan

The affirmative proposed that we increase income taxes for people with incomes over $200,000. However, these people are job creators. Increasing their taxes will cost jobs and harm the economy.

Furthermore, the affirmative provided no additional funding. When you raise taxes, more enforcement will be needed, which costs money.

...

In conclusion, I urge the judges to REJECT the resolution, "Taxes should be increased." Thank you. I am now ready for cross-examination.

ADVANTAGES

Every debater should stand in front of the room and read:

Are the judges ready? Is the timer ready?

Good morning. My name is [your name], and my partner, [partner's name], and I stand AGAINST the resolution: "Taxes should be increased."

Observation 1: Definitions

The negative accepts the affirmative's definitions.

Observation 2: Harms

Harm 1: The affirmative team said that schools are underfunded, BUT schools pay a lot of money per student and still fail.

> QUOTE: "The public schools in Washington, DC spent $29,349 per pupil in the 2010–2011 school year, according to the latest data from National Center for Education Statistics, but in 2013, fully 83 percent of the eighth graders in these schools were not 'proficient' in reading and 81 percent were not 'proficient' in math." END QUOTE
>
> SOURCE: Terence P. Jeffrey, CNSNews.com, May 14, 2014.
>
> SUMMARY: A lack of money is not the issue—poorly used resources is.

Harm 2: The affirmative team said that poor people need more health care, BUT, again, a lack of money is not the issue—poorly used resources are.

Observation 3: Plan

The affirmative proposed that we increase income taxes for people with incomes over $200,000. However, these people are job creators. Increasing their taxes will cost jobs and harm the economy.

Furthermore, the affirmative provided no additional funding. When you raise taxes, more enforcement will be needed, which costs money.

Observation 4: Advantages

Advantage 1: The affirmative said we will have more resources for schools, BUT the school system is fundamentally broken.

> SUMMARY: If the DC school systems can't succeed with $29,000 per student, throwing money at the problem isn't going to make it better.

Advantage 2: The affirmative said people will be healthier, BUT increasing taxes will harm more people than it helps.

> QUOTE: "Lower taxes, smaller government, and freedom to trade will better the lives of all Americans...." END QUOTE
>
> SOURCE: Representative Kevin Brady (R-TX), Heritage Foundation release of the 2016 Index of Economic Freedom, Feb. 1, 2016.
>
> SUMMARY: We need to create real economic growth in order to provide better services to Americans.

In conclusion, I urge the judges to REJECT the resolution, "Taxes should be increased." Thank you. I am now ready for cross-examination.

Congratulations! You have just completed a Negative Constructive speech.

Notice that only one of the quotations used is specific to the affirmative's case (the one about school spending). The rest could have been found just knowing the resolution. Would this case have been stronger if the negative speaker had evidence dealing with both health care and school spending? Yes. Did the negative speaker do a good job challenging the affirmative case with the evidence she had? Yes.

When you look at a Negative Constructive as a combination of generic research in opposition to the resolution, good probing questions, and a few specific arguments against the affirmative case, it becomes much easier. When debaters are just starting out, most of the hard work can be done ahead of time.

TEAM STRATEGIES

The negative team doesn't need to defeat every point of the affirmative team's case. But they can't get away with demonstrating that just one piece of evidence is weak. Their strategy should be to concentrate on defeating one or more large element ("observation") in the affirmative's case. The negative team's choices are:

1. **Definitions** — The affirmative might have weak, biased, or insignificant definitions. If the audience doesn't understand what is being argued, the affirmative has failed to set up the case properly.
2. **Harms** — The affirmative might have described harms that are insignificant or are anecdotal or out of the jurisdiction of policy makers. If this is the case, then there is no reason for a debate and the affirmative team has failed to set up the case properly.
3. **Plan/Solution** — Maybe the definitions are solid and the harms are real, but the solution will obviously not correct the problem. The solution could be too expensive or unenforceable. Again, the affirmative has failed to set up the case properly.
4. **Advantages** — If any of the three first observations can be attacked, it is worth reminding the audience that the advantages are just smoke and mirrors since we will never have them.

CONSIDERING THE STOCK ISSUES

As the affirmative team plans their case, they need to consider four important aspects of any policy change. These four are often called **stock issues** by debaters. The negative team will use these issues to assess the weaknesses of the affirmative case. Beginning debaters might not call the stock issues by name, and that's okay.

STOCK ISSUES
Four major issues that the affirmative must prove and the negative may attack.

SIGNIFICANCE
Whether or not the affirmative's HARMS or ADVANTAGES are important.

INHERENCY
Whether or not the affirmative's HARMS are caused by the current policy and thus can be fixed by changing it.

Significance

Policy shouldn't be changed if there is no important or large reason to do so, or if few people are affected by it (it could seem important, but only to a small number of people). Legislators try not to waste time on small things. Policies should change things significantly. For example, you wouldn't change a whole library system because of one poorly written book or one evil librarian or one computer crashing the catalog system for a day. These are examples of problems that people just have to deal with, not make new laws to correct.

Inherency

Inherency is tough to explain because most people argue emotionally and locally, rather than rationally with broad knowledge. For example, let's say that the government wants to make a policy change to reduce school bus accidents. They decide that the problem is the visibility of the buses, so they address the problem by assigning specific colors to buses, and adding lights, stop signs, and lots of speeding regulations. Unfortunately, the buses now move so slowly that they cause more accidents in general traffic. This solution ignored the real problem, which is that most buses don't have seatbelts, thanks to an early study suggesting that seatbelts were ineffective in buses. Lots of research and policy making were directed at things that logically seemed effective but really weren't the problem. Inherency helps us to assess cause and effect, allowing us to match problems to the correct solution.

Topicality

The resolution is intended to set reasonable boundaries for the debate so that everyone in the debate is talking about the same thing. For example, let's say the resolution is, "The United States Federal Government should reform its immigration policy." If the affirmative team proposed to make immigrants ineligible for welfare, the negative team could argue that this is not topical because welfare is a state issue and not the jurisdiction of the federal government.

Solvency

Solvency assesses whether or not the plan the affirmative team has proposed will actually fix the problems they have identified. For example, a debate about genetically modified foods might be trying to solve the problem of ill-informed consumers. The affirmative team might propose additional labelling requirements for genetically modified foods. The negative team might argue that this won't solve the problem because no one reads the labels already on foods.

Remember, a good affirmative case SITS solidly on all four stock issues, and a good negative team tries to call into question at least one of these issues.

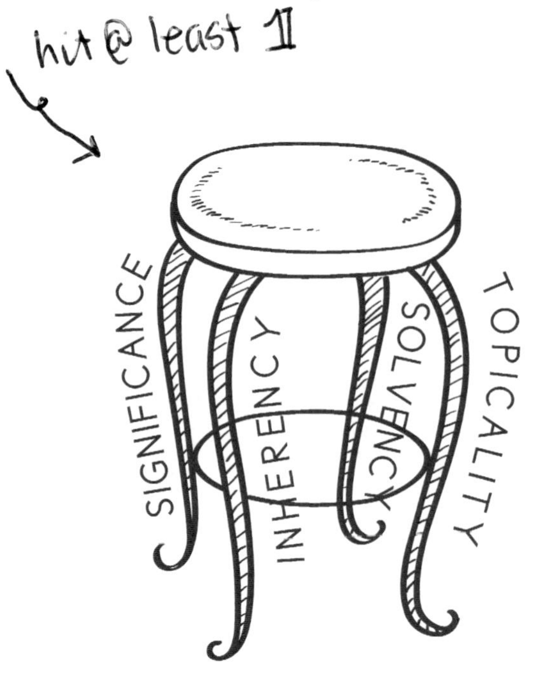

TOPICALITY
: Whether or not the affirmative case stays within the boundaries of the RESOLUTION.

SOLVENCY
: Whether or not the affirmative case will solve the HARMS it has identified.

The Rebuttals: Bringing It Home

The rebuttal is difficult for beginning debaters because it is fairly formless and it's the last thing a debater does in the debate. Keep the rebuttal last: last to practice and last in the debate outline. Researching and writing a good constructive case well will lead to a better understanding of rebuttals. The following are forms that aid to the construction of a good rebuttal.

Think about a rebuttal in terms of ancient architecture: Poorly braced roofs, and later the height of cathedrals and castles, created enormous outward pressure on the building materials, so architects added **buttresses**, sloping support structures that diffused the pressure on the walls. Likewise, while your rebuttal should address the other team's case, its most important purpose is to shore up your constructive arguments against the pressure the other team has applied.

A persuasive rebuttal begins with good research before the debate. Preparation leaves you with plenty of enthusiasm for your points. A rebuttal is your chance to demonstrate that you understand the opponent's points, that you really listened and thought about what they said, but it wasn't enough. You can still easily refute them.

A beginning debater often does well through the constructive speeches and cross-examinations, only to become exhausted when it's time to quickly prepare a rebuttal from notes taken. Having fresh evidence or analogies will reinvigorate you and the judges. The extra evidence will help you to think on your feet. Your rebuttal will allude to all the previous good points but will seem fresh, rather than rehashed.

The rebuttal should consider these three points of attitude:

1. You're grateful that the teams and judges have come together for the good of policy making.
2. Your opponents have presented specific information and arguments (even if they did it poorly).
3. Your proposal is still the better policy for our citizens when you weigh the evidence on both sides.

Therefore,

1. you still open and conclude your rebuttal with introductions and thanks,
2. you briefly restate your opponents' points and your responses to them, and then

REBUTTAL
: A shorter speech that summarizes the arguments made in the CONSTRUCTIVES and argues for the superiority of the speaker's side.

3. spend the majority of your time on your best argument, rebuilding your case and leaving a strong impression on the judge.

TEAM STRATEGIES

Imagine the judge's perspective as you assess what you need to do in your last speeches to persuade the judge of your argument.

Is it a…	In other words…	Then why not…?
Disagreement based on FACTS or LOGIC (***logos***)?	"If the judge KNEW this fact, he would understand why my case is stronger."	Present a statistic.
	"If the judge UNDERSTOOD this argument, she would support my case."	Explain your argument.
Disagreement based on CREDIBILITY (***ethos***)?	"If the judge TRUSTED my sources, he would understand why my case is stronger."	Share credentials or a corroborating source.
Disagreement based on EMOTION (***pathos***)?	"If the judge FELT the significance of this, she would understand why my case is stronger."	Tell a story.

Even when the debaters are not speaking, they should be actively engaged in the debate, both taking notes and preparing for the next speeches.

LOGOS
An appeal to logic.

ETHOS
An appeal to ethics.

PATHOS
An appeal to emotion.

THE BASICS OF TEAM POLICY DEBATE

The Debater's Role While Listening

Taking Notes with a Flow Chart

Flow-charting is a verb to debaters just like it is to computer programmers and project managers. Flow-charting is the art of making very brief notes in organized columns to ensure all four debaters are tracking one another in a debate. There are a few different versions. It's okay to teach one form, but debaters will eventually morph the form to the way they think. New debaters often get so caught up in listening to the debate that they forget to take notes and then forget arguments later.

It is the sign of a seasoned intellect to be able to listen, think, and write all at the same time. Flow-charting hones this skill. Debate has many benefits for students, not the least of which is note-taking practice. If you're debating with a partner who needs to read your handwriting, you have extra incentive to write neatly and quickly. Students who wish to practice this outside of debate can practice by taking notes to their pastor's sermon each week. They should try to identify the thesis and the strongest and weakest points used in its defense.

During the debate, students usually use long legal pads to "flow" the round. They divide the pad into a number of columns with a ruled line. The first column lists the particulars of debate that a team is listening for: definitions, harms, plan, and advantages. Each subsequent column is a space for notes from each speech (1AC, 1NC, 2AC, etc.). Some use symbols to keep notes, others write single words, most mix mediums. For example, if Definitions, Harm A, Harm B, Mandate, Agency, Enforcement, Advantage A, and Advantage B are listed in the first column, the flow-charter may put a one-word reminder like "death," "taxes," or "10%" to remember the argument given.

Some students include a column for cross-examination, and some just keep a sticky pad for cross-examination questions so they can hand them to their partner to use. Students can also put sticky notes into be put into their own speeches so they remember new ideas to argue as they are listening. Others fold up the bottom of the page to form matching columns that can be used to write questions. No matter how you do it, ideally, by the end of the debate an outsider should be able to follow each line of argument across the chart, left to right, from beginning to end.

FLOW CHART
A notepad used during a debate to trace arguments across each speech. See also FLOWING.

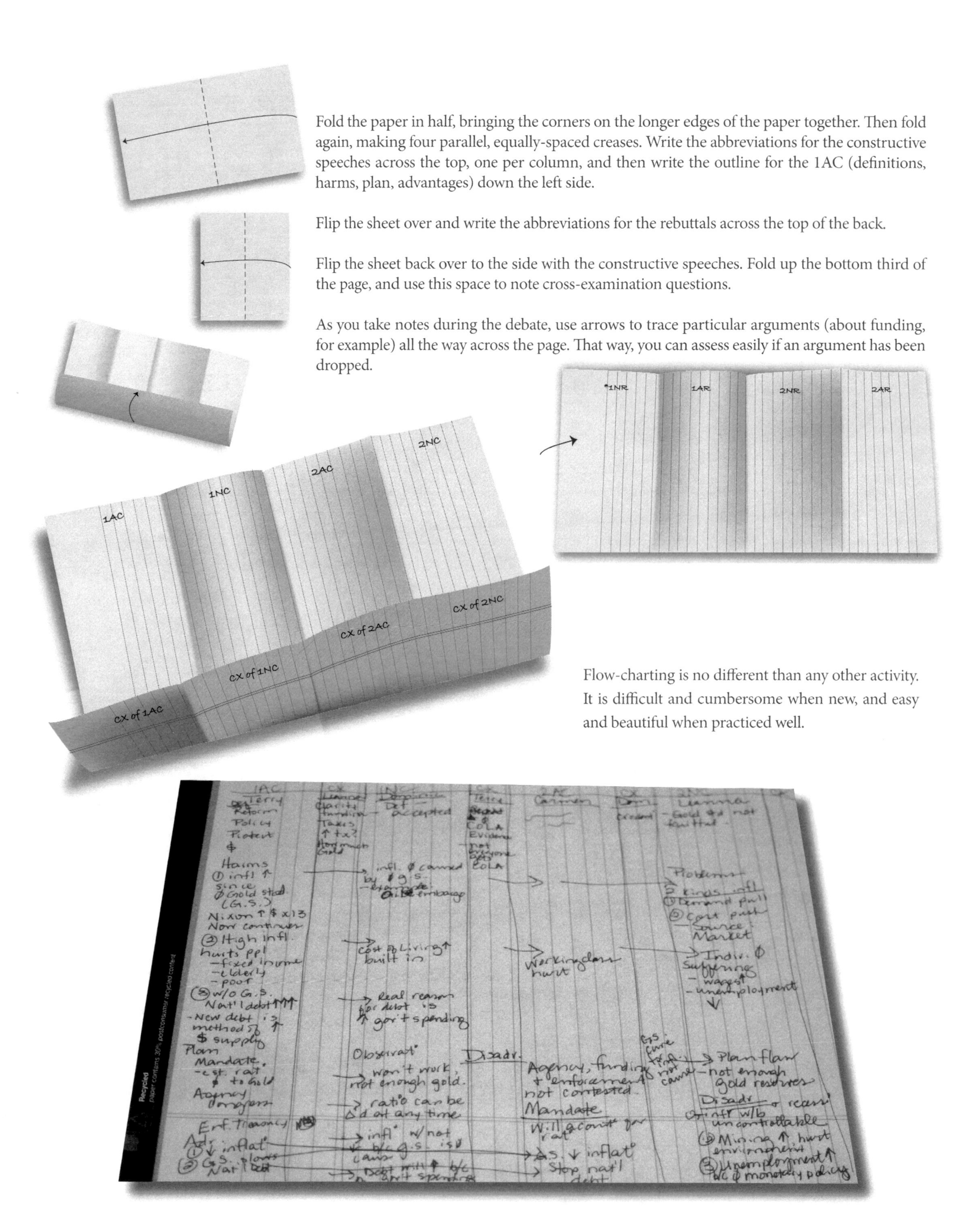

Fold the paper in half, bringing the corners on the longer edges of the paper together. Then fold again, making four parallel, equally-spaced creases. Write the abbreviations for the constructive speeches across the top, one per column, and then write the outline for the 1AC (definitions, harms, plan, advantages) down the left side.

Flip the sheet over and write the abbreviations for the rebuttals across the top of the back.

Flip the sheet back over to the side with the constructive speeches. Fold up the bottom third of the page, and use this space to note cross-examination questions.

As you take notes during the debate, use arrows to trace particular arguments (about funding, for example) all the way across the page. That way, you can assess easily if an argument has been dropped.

Flow-charting is no different than any other activity. It is difficult and cumbersome when new, and easy and beautiful when practiced well.

Preparing for Upcoming Speeches

1AC

1. Second Affirmative listens well. If the 1AC runs out of time, misses a key point, or misspeaks (says something like "didn't" when he meant "did"), the Second Affirmative has to quickly prepare to recover when it is her turn to speak.
2. First Negative listens well and makes a flow chart. Everyone should be quiet during speeches—minimize whispering! If a listening debater needs to communicate with his partner, he can pass her a sticky note. Second Negative listens well and writes clarifying questions in preparation for cross-examination.

CX OF 1A BY 2N

1. First Negative reads the plan and chooses evidence from her printed research (more on this later) to counter points made. This requires quick thinking and organized evidence.
2. Second Affirmative listens to questions and begins to pull evidence to refute possible problems or shore up evidence given.

PREP TIME

1. First and Second Affirmative confer on flaws to overcome and pull evidence needed.
2. First and Second Negative quickly find evidence to counter each point of the case. They have never heard this case before, so now they have to scramble to argue.

1NC

1. Second Negative listens well. If the 1NC runs out of time, misses a key point, or misspeaks, the Second Negative has to quickly prepare to recover when it is his turn to speak.
2. First Affirmative listens well and writes clarifying questions.
3. Second Affirmative listens well and inserts notes into her flow chart that counter what she is listening to.

CX OF 1N BY 1A

1. Second Affirmative listens and pulls evidence to counter points made on the flow chart.
2. Second Negative listens to questions and pulls evidence to refute possible problems or shore up evidence given.

PREP TIME

1. First and Second Affirmative confer on flaws to overcome and pull evidence needed.

2. First and Second Negative quickly find evidence to counter each point of the case. They have begun to understand this case, so now they must strengthen their points of attack.

2AC

1. First Affirmative listens well. If the 2AC makes an error, the First Affirmative has to help recover during the rebuttals.
2. First Negative listens well and writes clarifying questions.
3. Second Negative listens well and inserts notes into his speech that counter what he is listening to.

CX OF 2A BY 1N

1. Second Negative listens and pulls evidence to counter points made on the flow chart to use in rebuttal.
2. First Affirmative listens to questions and pulls evidence that will clinch the affirma tive team's points in the rebuttal.

PREP TIME

1. First and Second Affirmative confer on flaws to overcome and pull evidence needed.
2. First and Second Negative quickly find evidence to counter each point of the case. They have begun to understand this case, so now they must strengthen their points of attack.

2NC

1. First Negative listens well. After the break, the First Negative speaks.
2. First Affirmative listens well and adds notes to flow chart to prepare for rebuttal.
3. Second Affirmative listens well and adds notes to flow chart to prepare for rebuttal.

CX OF 2N BY 2A

1. First Negative listens and begins to summarize the major points of the debate for the first rebuttal.
2. First Affirmative listens to questions and begins to prepare responses for the rebuttals.

PREP TIME*

1. First and Second Affirmative confer on rebuttals.
2. First and Second Negative confer on rebuttals.

1NR

1. All listen and add notes to flow chart to refute. You are still a team; pass notes to the bitter end!

PREP TIME*

1. First and Second Affirmative confer on rebuttals.
2. First and Second Negative confer on rebuttals.

1AR

1. All listen and add notes to flow chart to refute.

PREP TIME*

1. First and Second Affirmative confer on rebuttals.
2. First and Second Negative confer on rebuttals.

2NR

1. All listen and add notes to flow chart to refute.

PREP TIME*

1. First and Second Affirmative confer on rebuttals.
2. First and Second Negative confer on rebuttals.

2AR

1. All listen and shake hands when finished!

*If the speakers choose not to use prep time, or if the team has run out by this point, skip this step.

THE BASICS OF TEAM POLICY DEBATE

The Debater's Role While Researching

Now that we've covered what happens during the debate, let's talk about what happens before the debate. Research is a skill that takes time to develop. Be patient, and do not expect in-depth knowledge of the resolution the first time around. To prepare, the affirmative team should meet and write out their entire case in detail: both partner's constructive arguments, both cross-examination questions, and both rebuttals. Their constructive cases should be identical in outlined points and definitions with one exception—evidence and sources. As a team they are making the same point, but as two presenters they get the chance to present twice the evidence from experts.

The negative team does not know what the affirmative's specific case will be, but the resolution gives them a sense of the possible avenues for research. The negative also have an advantage: they only have to disprove one part of the affirmative case to win. The affirmative team has to defend every argument they make. As the negative do their research, they will come across recurring themes. Know a few arguments very well, and when it comes up in the affirmative's case, make that the point of attack. Understanding basic principles will make your job easier. The history of the policy in a previous time or setting could be your best argument against change. For example, "We've already fought in that country five times in the last hundred years, so why would a sixth war be a good idea?" or "We've already tried laissez-faire government and saw the rise of the wealthy few, so why do you think the free market works?"

Both teams should be prepared to present either position, negative or affirmative. This guarantees that they fully understand both sides of the argument.

Gathering Evidence

When you begin to research, start general rather than researching a particular side of an argument. This will help you to avoid biased evidence. Good places to start are newspaper articles, think tanks, books, and scholarly research from universities or published journals. As you go, divide your research into two categories: research that supports the resolution and research that negates it. You're looking for quotations, statistics, and examples that will help you make your case. From these cards and documents will come cross-examination questions, unscripted speeches, and rebuttals.

When you print and file this evidence for future use, be sure to include:

1. The point the quotation or statistic proves (often called a **tagline**)
2. The actual quotation or statistic
3. Information about the source and its credentials (date, sponsor, author, title)
4. A longer explanation in your own words explaining the relevance of quote

TAGLINE
A brief statement naming your point [harm,advantage,contention].

If the quotation is really good, it can serve as the explanation also. But some debate resolutions are complicated, so you'll need to use your own words to explain a point to the audience. This takes the most time, but it is also the most effective way to engage the judges because it demonstrates that you really understand your case and aren't just reading it.

For example:

Tagline: Banning Christmas carols before Thanksgiving would increase shopping.

Quote: "People who have been avoiding the mall before Thanksgiving would reappear."

Source: Mall Statisticians, "What's Driving Traffic Away in November?" Oct. 2015.

Explanation: Fear and loathing of Christmas carols has been driving shoppers away from the malls in November. Once we ban Christmas carols, the shoppers will come back.

TAG: Cats live completely indoors.

QUOTE: "Cats don't need to be walked outside and would most likely lie down and refuse to budge anyway."

SOURCE: Cato Sockscrates, Professor of Feline Philosophy at School of Athens, "Cat Autonomy." The Complete Philosophy of Cats. Athens: Agora Press, 429 BC. Print.

SUMMARY: Cats can fulfill all of their needs indoors, eliminating the need to go outside to be walked or do

As you research the affirmative case, you and your partner should find two to four pieces of evidence for each point of your case: one piece for each of your constructives and one piece for each of your rebuttals. This is an easy way for a beginner to be sure she is ready with lots of evidence.

You should also find two pieces of evidence against your case that reflect the negative of your point. When you are finished with the rough draft of your constructive, look at this evidence again and see if it makes your case look weak. Use it to think through the arguments your opponent might bring up against you. Put your points in an outline alongside your opponent's possible arguments. Use the notes to build a case against yourself. It will help you think like your opponent. Take those notes to help you plan your defense during the debate.

Write all of these pieces of evidence on notecards or print them on a document and file either by topic or by debate outline.

Assessing Your Evidence

To ensure that debaters are arguing fairly and honestly, they should assess research carefully. A handy memory trick is to **perform CPR** on your evidence. That means, ask, "Is it **C**redible? Is it **P**ublished? Is it **R**ecent?" Let's look at each of those criteria individually.

Credible: Evidence should be as credible and unbiased as possible. The people you quote should have some level of experience or expertise in the matter about which they are speaking. Biases should be carefully explained or acknowledged. Attacking one piece of evidence shouldn't be a substitute for arguing an entire point, but if all of your evidence is one-sided, it might appear that you didn't do your research.

Published: More information than ever is available on the Internet. Anyone can state an opinion or share a statistic—real or falsified. To ensure honest clash, a good principle is to quote primarily published (meaning vetted) sources: newspaper articles, research from think tanks, books, and scholarly papers. In most cases, it's difficult to verify that someone has fact-checked a blog.

Recent: For both teams, the evidence should be as current as possible, although it is fine to present it in the context of the history of the problem. Winston Churchill may provide an inspirational opening or closing quote, but try to use someone living for statistical evidence in the middle of your case. Aim for a maximum of three years old for statistics (government agencies don't conduct certain surveys every year), and be aware of political or social changes that might negate an older piece of evidence.

You can use those same questions to undermine your opponent's evidence during cross-examination. Then, use the other team's evidence in your rebuttal by pointing out a specific weakness in their evidence and then contrasting it with your own strong evidence.

INTRODUCTION TO Lincoln-Douglas Debate

Although the practice of debating ideals is centuries old, Lincoln-Douglas debates, also known as values debates, are named for a series of talks held in Illinois in 1858 between Abraham Lincoln and Stephen A. Douglas. Both men were running for the U.S. Senate and had clashed on the issue of slavery's expansion in the United States. Douglas argued that popular sovereignty should be the value that governed decisions about slavery, while Lincoln argued in favor of national unity as a governing principle. As this example shows, Lincoln-Douglas (often abbreviated "LD") debate is about philosophical principles and values. It goes one step deeper than policy debate because it assesses the principles that should govern our courses of action, either as individuals or as a community.

Middle school is a good time to begin teaching parts of LD debate by asking "should" questions about literature and current events, reading papers in front of an audience, practicing eye contact, and connecting with the audience while speaking.

High school students who are ready to study the different worldviews that have shaped science, government, art, music, and philosophy will find Lincoln-Douglas debate to be an outlet where they can discuss and debate the values that govern our decisions.

The Players' Roles

Judges

As in team policy debate, Lincoln-Douglas speakers are not trying to persuade each other; therefore, students learn to direct their speeches to an impartial judge or judges. This helps each debater argue the resolution rather than attack the other.

During the debate, the judge should take good notes while listening carefully to each speaker. The first responsibility of the judge is not to declare winners and losers; it is to provide feedback that will help both students improve. The judge should provide verbal or written assessment of lines of argument, questions and answers, persuasiveness, and public speaking skills.

Basic, healthy beginning models for assessment should focus more on progress than on winning. (Please review the "Spirit of Debate" section at the beginning of the book.) There are many ways you can give assessment well. It is not necessary to use a specific competition and judge's form unless you are preparing students to be competitive. The judges' forms are more often used when a person from outside the group needs a form of communication for a competition. The appendices include a sample assessment tool that focuses instead on the skills taught in formal debate.

Lincoln-Douglas judges should take the same view as our Father in Heaven. He is pleased with our best as we take the forms He gives us and fill them with appropriate, honoring content. Our assessments should not be used to say, "You were better than she was." Instead, they should inform the students what the judge was persuaded and pleased by and what could be improved.

Any students who are not participating in the debate should practice judging, too, because each day they must weigh the consequences of their own actions, watch out for snares from others, and one day judge principalities with their Brother, our Savior.

Timers

Lincoln-Douglas debates are timed events. Each portion of each debate requires a timer. Use the timer role to introduce a new student to the flow of Lincoln-Douglas debate or as a specific role if you have an uneven number of students in your debate class. The timer can be a single person or a different person for each side. The timer can be a parent, student, or tutor.

Timing is easy to do and simply requires the timer to pay attention to the sequence of speeches. Each part of a debate has a different amount of time, so a timer quickly learns the order of the debate. Often the timer acts as facilitator of a debate because his job is to make sure the right person is speaking in the right order for the correct amount of time.

Setting the timer and nodding when ready are the main tasks. The timer should count down for the speaker by raising the appropriate number of fingers to indicate the number of minutes the speaker has left: five at the five-minute mark, four at the four-minute mark, and so on. It is also helpful if he can put fingers up at 10 seconds left and count backwards to "time's up."

Below is a sample schedule so debaters know how much time to prepare for. The times are arbitrary and can be shortened for practice in class. Serious competitors will want to practice speeches for these lengths of time:

- Affirmative Constructive: 6 minutes
- Cross-Examination: 3 minutes
- Negative Constructive: 7 minutes
- Cross-Examination: 3 minutes
- First Affirmative Rebuttal: 4 minutes
- Negative Rebuttal: 6 minutes
- Second Affirmative Rebuttal: 3 minutes

You might notice that the constructive speeches are not the same length, and neither are the rebuttals. This is a math lesson waiting to happen! Both speakers should get the same amount of total speaking time, but the affirmative goes first and last, so:

6 + 3 + 4 + 3 (Affirmative) = 3 + 7 + 6 (Negative)

The timer is also responsible for keeping track of preparation ("prep") time in between speeches. Each speaker is given a certain amount of prep time for the entire debate round and treats it like a bank account, withdrawing amounts of prep time before each speech. For example, your class or debate club may give a total of five minutes of prep time per speaker. If a speaker wants two minutes to prepare, she must inform the timer, who keeps track of all the prep minutes and tells the speaker when her prep time has been exhausted.

Coaches and Facilitators

The debate facilitator and the judge are often the same person. A coach or facilitator does not need to be an expert to begin coaching debate. This resource, as well as hundreds online, can help the coach improve right along with the students. New coaches need to be given the same grace to fail as new students. The only qualification needed is the willingness to learn debate and to help the debaters learn one step at a time. This guide is designed just for you.

A QUICK CHECKLIST OF THINGS TO TEACH LINCOLN-DOUGLAS DEBATERS

1. Introduce yourself and conclude with a reminder of the resolution.
2. Think of values that are important for society to uphold.

3. Brainstorm a few ways to measure those abstract values concretely.
4. Research the reasons those values are important.
5. Think through both sides of the resolution, even if you disagree with one.
6. Stand in front of an audience while making eye contact.
7. Find more advanced debate material if you are enjoying debate.

In Lincoln-Douglas debate, the facilitator needs a minimum of two students, one per side. A debate can take 45 minutes to complete if you keep to competition times, making it difficult for a facilitator with more than two students. Below are suggestions for additional students:

> Three: The third student is a timer, judge, critic, or possibly all three. The third student should also prepare an AC in order to practice and to be prepared to substitute if needed.
>
> Four: Two rounds of debate. Times can be shortened to fit the time available.
>
> Five: Two rounds, and the role of the third student above.

Any more students will fall into one of the above combinations.

Debaters

Lincoln-Douglas debate has two roles for debaters: affirmative and negative. Each speaker gets to present at least two speeches, listen to the other speaker, and ask and answer cross-examination questions. Later, we'll talk about the different responsibilities of each of these speakers.

The practiced debater learns to listen and withhold arguments and judgments until the opponent has concluded, learns to uncover the underlying assumptions of an argument, learns to respect the ideas of others, and learns to separate form from content. Formal debating teaches us to respect the art of thinking through questioning, reasoning, researching, and presenting. Only some people will love debate, but all can benefit from the practice of Lincoln-Douglas debate.

A N

The Resolution

In Lincoln-Douglas debate, the resolution sets the bounds of the debate. A person of influence (a pastor, a politician, a doctor, a lawyer, a judge) believes we should act in a certain way, based on our values. Clarity makes the difference between productive argument (the two parties actually disagree on a fundamental level) and pure arguing (the two parties are talking past one another).

Although the form of resolutions in Lincoln-Douglas debate varies more than it does in team policy debate, you can expect to see some form of "should" statement, or an expression of moral obligation similar to:

"Resolved: This group should / should not / has a moral obligation to behave in a certain way."

Examples include:

1. Resolved: People should be willing to risk their lives to rescue cultural artifacts.
2. Resolved: The U.S. government has a moral obligation to assist in global health crises.
3. Resolved: Democracies ought to value free speech more highly than public safety.

The resolution should clearly state the topic for debate and permit two clear positions ("should" and "should not") but be broad enough to encourage research and thought. It is the affirmative speaker's job to promote or agree with the resolution. It is the negative speaker's job to reject or disagree with the resolution.

New debaters often think that the negative speaker must argue the opposite extreme of the resolution. This is not necessary. In the second example, the negative speaker does not need to argue that the U.S. government has a moral obligation **not to** assist in global health crises. Instead, he responds directly to the affirmative's claim by arguing that the United States does not have a moral obligation to assist. The difference is subtle, but it goes a long way toward preventing debates from devolving into shouting matches in which both sides ignore what the other person is saying.

THE BASICS OF LINCOLN-DOUGLAS DEBATE

The Debater's Role While Speaking

Lincoln-Douglas debate is an orderly argument between two people. It is similar to a scene from a play with a script. The script in Appendix 5 is a silly example of a full Lincoln-Douglas debate. Debate classes can read the script aloud together to give the debaters a general idea of what they are about to learn.

This next section will examine what happens in each part of the debate, so you may want to read the sample script before continuing. Details and descriptions that add to the debate form will be explained in the next section. This is meant to be read aloud to give debaters a general idea of what they are about to learn.

AFFIRMATIVE CONSTRUCTIVE

A person who wants to make a moral claim:

1. Introduces herself.
2. Defines some terms.
3. Names the value at stake in this situation.
4. Explains how we will know when the value has been upheld.
5. Lists several reasons why the moral claim is valid.
6. Concludes by asking the audience to affirm the moral claim.

In a values debate, just like in team policy debate, this speech is called the AC or Affirmative Constructive because it constructs (builds) the foundations of the argument in favor of the resolution.

CROSS-EXAMINATION

A person who doesn't agree with the moral claim has been listening and thinking about what the first person has just shared. Now he gets a chance to ask the affirmative speaker some questions, called cross-examination. The questioner asks for clarification on the points made by the first person. It would be silly to argue against a case that you don't understand, so these questions tend to be very basic.

1. Would you please repeat your definition?
2. Why is this value the most important one to consider?

3. What evidence did you use to prove that this moral claim is valid?

In summary, the affirmative introduced a moral claim. Then the negative cross-examined the affirmative for clarity on the argument.

NEGATIVE CONSTRUCTIVE

The person who doesn't agree with the moral claim (the negative) now gets to build his own case against the resolution. After he does that, he must also address each argument or point the affirmative made.

The person who doesn't agree with the moral claim:

1. Introduces himself.
2. Defines terms he will use, especially if he thinks a term should be defined differently.
3. Accepts the value at stake or proposes a different one (both debaters can name the same value but use different standards for measuring it).
4. Offers different standards to show when the value has been met.
5. Lists several reasons why the moral claim is not valid.
6. Responds directly to each of the other speaker's arguments.
7. Concludes by asking the audience to reject the moral claim.

In a Lincoln-Douglas debate, this speech is called the NC or Negative Constructive because it constructs (builds) the foundations of the argument in opposition to the resolution.

CROSS-EXAMINATION

The person who began the debate, the affirmative, now gets to ask questions in return. Fair is fair! This is the affirmative's chance not only to clear up misunderstandings with the negative but also to ask questions to help the judge or judges see problems with the current situation, which the negative has just defended.

The affirmative might cross-examine the negative like this:

1. Did you accept the definitions?
2. Why do you think your standards are a better way to measure the value?
3. What evidence did you use to prove that the claim was not valid?

In summary, the affirmative introduced a moral claim. The negative cross-examined the affirmative for clarity on the argument. The negative made a case that the moral claim is not valid. Then the affirmative cross-examined the negative for clarity on the argument.

FIRST AFFIRMATIVE REBUTTAL

Now the audience has heard both sides of the argument. It is the affirmative speaker's turn again, but she cannot simply repeat arguments, ignoring what the negative speaker has said. Instead, she must synthesize what both sides have said, to demonstrate how her argument is stronger. The affirmative speaker:

1. Reminds the audience who she is.
2. Briefly reviews any arguments about definitions.
3. Explains why her value, not the negative's, is most important.
4. Reiterates her standard (called a **criterion**) for meeting that value.
5. Refutes each argument made by the opposing speaker.
6. Explains why her arguments are still valid in light of what the other speaker has said.
7. Concludes by asking the judge or judges to affirm the moral claim—the resolution.

NEGATIVE REBUTTAL

The negative must now tie together everything that has been said in a way that will help the judges see that the affirmative has not made a strong enough argument for the moral claim. This is the negative's last chance to speak, so he must focus most of his attention on the strongest arguments against the affirmative case. The negative speaker:

1. Reminds the judges and audience who he is.
2. Identifies the key points of disagreement between the negative and affirmative positions.
3. Shows why the negative's value is more important.
4. Shows the flaws in the affirmative's standards.
5. Explains why his arguments are stronger in light of what the other speaker has said.
6. Concludes by asking the judges to reject the moral claim in the resolution.

SECOND AFFIRMATIVE REBUTTAL

The affirmative speaker gets the last word in the debate round. It has been a heated debate, but a civil one. The affirmative came in believing in the importance of her moral claim. She has discovered some points of clarification through argument, but she still feels strongly that her value is a good basis for decision-making and personal or political action. Now she must remind the listeners of the bigger picture.

In this final speech, she:

1. Reminds the judges who she is.
2. Identifies the key points of disagreement between the negative and affirmative positions.
3. Provides additional support for the importance of her value.
4. Confirms that her moral claim will meet the standards she has outlined.
5. Reminds the judges what is at stake if the moral claim is not upheld.
6. Concludes by asking the judges to affirm the resolution.

CRITERION/CRITERIA
The standard(s) used to measure whether or not a VALUE has been met.

The Debater's Role While Speaking: Double Time!

As we've just seen, each debater gets to construct a case, cross-examine an opponent, take notes, prepare, and give at least one rebuttal. The process of just standing to present at the proper time is important to practice.

Using this outline, have both debaters walk through their roles until they can do so without looking at the outline. This is very important to practice so the debaters can do so without thinking. They have enough to think about.

A stands and says:
"AC — First Affirmative Constructive"

N joins the A and both say:
"Cross-Examination of AC by N"

A and N sit, pause; N stands and says:
"NC — Negative Constructive"

A joins the N and both say:
"Cross-Examination of NC by A"

A and N sit, pause; A stands and says:
"1AR — First Affirmative Rebuttal"

A sits, N stands and says:
"NR — Negative Rebuttal"

N sits, A stands and says:
"2AR – Second Affirmative Rebuttal"

Notice that the affirmative speaks first and last. It might appear that this gives the affirmative an advantage, but the Negative Constructive is longer than the Affirmative Constructive. The Negative Constructive is really two speeches in one: a combination of a constructive and a first rebuttal. We'll talk more about this later.

The Affirmative Constructive in Lincoln-Douglas Debate

Now that we have outlined the general elements that belong in each speech of a Lincoln-Douglas debate, it's time to delve into the details, using a concrete example to help students master the form and the vocabulary. We'll start with the very first speech, the Affirmative Constructive.

INTRODUCTION, RESOLUTION, AND CONCLUSION

Every debater should stand in front of the room and read:

> Are the judges ready? Is the timer ready?
>
> Good morning. My name is [your name], and I stand FOR the resolution: "Democracies ought to value free speech more highly than public safety."
>
> ...
>
> In conclusion, I urge the judges to AFFIRM the resolution, "Democracies ought to value free speech more highly than public safety." Thank you. I am now ready for cross-examination.

You have now used the form to open and close a Lincoln-Douglas constructive speech.

Now every debater should stand in front of the room and say the same thing without reading or notes. Say it from memory.

Next, every debater should stand in front of the room and say the same thing without reading or notes. Say it from memory, but change two words. Instead of "FOR" say "AGAINST" the resolution, and instead of "AFFIRM" say "REJECT" the resolution. This represents the negative position.

DEFINITIONS

Definitions can seem like a waste of time until you realize that most arguments are over definitions. What counts as art? What is a government's job? What does "free speech" mean? People who care about ideas also care about the words used to express the ideas, so we work to provide clarity.

Every debater should stand in front of the room and read.

> Are the judges ready? Is the timer ready?
>
> Good morning. My name is [your name], and I stand for the resolution: "Democracies ought to value free speech more highly than public safety."

Observation 1: Definitions

Democracy: "a government in which the supreme power is vested in the people.
Source: Merriam-Webster.com

Free speech: "the right of people to express their opinions publicly without government interference.
Source: Dictionary.com

Public safety: "the welfare and protection of the general public.
Source: USLegal.com

...

In conclusion, I urge the judges to AFFIRM the resolution, "Democracies ought to value free speech more highly than public safety." Thank you. I am now ready for cross-examination.

Let's evaluate what we just said:

- Why do we have to list sources for definitions?
- Are these legitimate sources?
- Why did we define some phrases instead of individual words?

VALUE

In a team policy debate, the teams are arguing over whether or not a policy change will address a problem. In a Lincoln-Douglas debate, the teams are arguing that one value has higher worth than another. In an LD round, the affirmative speaker sets a value that best upholds the resolution.

Every debater should stand in front of the room again and read:

Are the judges ready? Is the timer ready?

Good morning. My name is [your name], and I stand FOR the resolution: "Democracies ought to value free speech more highly than public safety."

Observation 1: Definitions

Democracy: "a government in which the supreme power is vested in the people.
Source: Merriam-Webster.com

Free speech: "the right of people to express their opinions publicly without government interference.
Source: Dictionary.com

Public safety: "the welfare and protection of the general public.
Source: USLegal.com

Observation 2: Value

Our value today is free speech.

...

In conclusion, I urge the judges to AFFIRM the resolution, "Democracies ought to value free speech more highly than public safety." Thank you. I am now ready for cross-examination.

Let's evaluate what we just said:

- What purpose does a value serve?
- Does the value always come directly from the resolution?
- Have we defined what "free speech" means?

CRITERION

Values are abstract, so we need some way to know whether or not we've fulfilled them. The criterion (plural, criteria) is the standard of measurement each speaker uses to determine whether or not the value has been met.

Every debater should stand in front of the room and read:

Are the judges ready? Is the timer ready?

Good morning. My name is [your name], and I stand for the resolution: "Democracies ought to value free speech more highly than public safety."

Observation 1: Definitions

Democracy: "a government in which the supreme power is vested in the people.
Source: Merriam-Webster.com

Free speech: "the right of people to express their opinions publicly without government interference.
Source: Dictionary.com

Public safety: "the welfare and protection of the general public.
Source: USLegal.com

Observation 2: Value

Our value today is free speech.

Observation 3: Criterion

The criterion we will use to measure free speech is lack of government censorship.

...

In conclusion, I urge the judges to affirm the resolution, "Democracies ought to value free speech more highly than public safety." Thank you. I am now ready for cross-examination.

Let's evaluate what we just said:

- What was our criterion (plural, criteria)?
- Does this criterion provide a good way to measure the value?
- Is there a better way to measure freedom of speech?

CONTENTIONS

The **contentions** will support the criterion. It might be helpful to think about the construction of the LD speeches by comparing them to the persuasive essay with which students are already familiar. The value is similar to the thesis. The criterion would be similar to a proof of the thesis, and the contentions would be similar to subproofs.

Every debater should stand in front of the room and read:

Are the judges ready? Is the timer ready?

Good morning. My name is [your name], and I stand FOR the resolution: "Democracies ought to value free speech more highly than public safety."

Observation 1: Definitions

Democracy: "a government in which the supreme power is vested in the people.
Source: Merriam-Webster.com

Free speech: "the right of people to express their opinions publicly without government interference.
Source: Dictionary.com

Public safety: "the welfare and protection of the general public.
Source: USLegal.com

Observation 2: Value

Our value today is free speech.

Observation 3: Criterion

The criterion we will use to measure free speech is lack of government censorship.

Observation 4: Contentions

Contention 1: Freedom of speech is essential to democracy.

QUOTE: "Freedom to think as you will and to speak as you think are means indispensable to the discovery and spread of political truth." END QUOTE

SOURCE: Justice Louis Brandeis, Whitney v. California (1927)

SUMMARY: Without freedom of speech, democracy cannot survive.

Contention 2: Politicians can use the claim of "public safety" to justify their own ends.

QUOTE: "Once a government is committed to the principle of silencing the voice of opposition, it has only one way to go, and that is down the path of increasingly repressive measures, until it becomes a source of terror to all its citizens and creates a country where everyone lives in fear." END QUOTE

SOURCE: President Harry Truman

SUMMARY: Valuing public safety over free speech is the same philosophy that led the Chinese to attack student protesters in Tiananmen Square in 1989.

Contention 3: Freedom of the press is necessary for government to be held accountable.

CONTENTION(S)
A specific reason or logical proof that your side of the RESOLUTION meets the CRITERION for upholding the VALUE.

QUOTE: "We named people in specific acts of participation in a criminal conspiracy essentially to destroy the free electoral system we have in this country to spy and sabotage on the Democrats." END QUOTE

SOURCE: Journalist Bob Woodward

SUMMARY: The Watergate scandal is a perfect example of why freedom of the press is essential for democracy's system of checks and balances.

In conclusion, I urge the judges to AFFIRM the resolution, "Democracies ought to value free speech more highly than public safety." Thank you. I am now ready for cross-examination.

Let's evaluate what we just said:

- What kind of evidence did we use to support these contentions?
- How are Lincoln-Douglas sources different from those used in team policy debate?
- Do the quotations prove what we say they do?
- Did you remember to say "Observation 2" and "Contention 1" and "Quote" and "Source" aloud? If not, go back and practice doing it that way.

Debates are timed, so to use time effectively, debaters use consistent words as indicators to abbreviate phrases. Instead of wasting time saying, "I got my information from…" they just say, "Source." Debaters say "quote" (and, sometimes, "end quote") aloud so their audience knows when they're using someone else's words. It's a matter of integrity—giving credit where credit is due.

Congratulations! You have now read an entire simple Affirmative Constructive for a Lincoln-Douglas debate. Thankfully for our negative speaker's sake, the case is not perfect: it leaves plenty of room for questions and disagreement.

The Negative Constructive in Lincoln-Douglas Debate

Unlike in team policy debate, the Negative Constructive in Lincoln-Douglas debate is a mix of pre-written and unscripted material. The negative speaker will have prepared his own value, criterion, and contentions ahead of time, aiming to argue against the resolution.

Now that he has heard the affirmative case, he may find that they agree on value but each has a different criterion for measuring it, or they may be arguing for different values. The negative speaker will present his own contentions negating the resolution and then argue against the affirmative's contentions.

Here is what a sample Negative Constructive might look like in outline form, distinguishing what is prepared ahead of time from what is inserted during prep time. The "**E**" indicates evidence (a quotation or statistic).

	Notes from AC	Neg prepared before debate	Neg added during prep
Resolution	Democracies ought to value free speech more highly than public safety	Democracies should NOT value free speech more highly than public safety	e.g., should value equally
Definitions	Democracies: power in people Free speech: express publicly, no interference Public safety: welfare and protection	[Negative prepares own definitions, ready to propose if needed]	Definitions are okay. Accept all.
Value	Free speech	Public safety	
Criterion	Lack of government censorship	Balance of freedom and reasonable restraints.	
Contentions	1. Essential to democracy 2. Safety = untrustworthy 3. Press as watchdog	1. Democracy < Voting < Public safety. 2. Government's first responsibility is to protect. 3. Constitution permits	Response to Aff Case 1. Safety first! (**E**) 2. Applies to both values 3. Safety first!

The negative would have brought his own case to the round, including a negative value, criterion, and contentions, and then planned his arguments against the affirmative's specific case while listening to the AC and during prep time.

Here is what that same Negative Constructive might look like in speech form:

> Are the judges ready? Is the timer ready?
>
> Good morning. My name is [your name], and I stand AGAINST the resolution: "Democracies ought to value free speech more highly than public safety."

Observation 1: Definitions

The negative accepts the affirmative's definitions.

Observation 2: Value

The affirmative's value was freedom of speech, but I propose that public safety is a higher value.

Observation 3: Criterion

Protection from harm or threat of harm

Observation 4: Contentions

Contention 1. Voting is essential to democracy, and public safety is essential to voting.

> QUOTE: "They cut off my hands and told me that I couldn't vote for democracy anymore. They don't like democracy.... I suffered for democracy, so I have to support democracy until the end of my life." END QUOTE
> SOURCE: "Sierra Leone: A Tale of Three Amputees," AllAfrica Global Media, 2002.
>
> SUMMARY: Rebels in Sierra Leone understood that one effective way to undermine democracy was to use threats and violence to prevent people from voting.

Contention 2. The government's first responsibility is to protect its citizens.

> QUOTE: "We the people of the United States, in order to form a more perfect union, establish justice, insure domestic tranquility, provide for the common defense, promote the general welfare, and secure the blessings of liberty to ourselves and our posterity, do ordain and establish this Constitution for the United States of America." END QUOTE
> SOURCE: Preamble to the Constitution
>
> SUMMARY: Insuring domestic tranquility, providing for the common defense, and promoting the general welfare are three of the purposes the Constitution sets out for the United States government.

Contention 3: The Constitution permits reasonable limitations on free speech.

> QUOTE: "First Amendment rights do not guarantee to the plaintiffs (or anyone else, for that matter) an interested, attentive, and receptive audience, available at close range. The right of the state to take reasonable steps to ensure the safe passage of persons wishing to enter health care facilities cannot seriously be questioned." END QUOTE
> SOURCE: U.S. Court of Appeals for the First Circuit, 2000
>
> SUMMARY: The court argued that the right to protest stops if it means preventing someone else from entering a health care facility.

Response to Affirmative Case

Contention 1: The affirmative said freedom of speech is essential to democracy, BUT,

> QUOTE: "What is the essence of democracy and multi-party politics if it still results in violence that leads to the destruction of life, livelihood, and property?" END QUOTE

SOURCE: Samuel Mondays Atuobi, Kofi Annan International Peacekeeping Training Centre

Contention 2: The affirmative said politicians use public safety to justify their own ends, BUT the same thing could be said about freedom of speech. Potential misuse does not make public safety less important.

Contention 3: The affirmative said freedom of the press holds government accountable, and that may be true, BUT that should not happen at the expense of public safety.

In conclusion, I urge the judges to REJECT the resolution, "Democracies ought to value free speech more highly than public safety." Thank you. I am now ready for cross-examination.

Remember, the negative's job is to argue AGAINST the resolution, rather than simply arguing FOR its opposite. Another approach to this example would have been arguing that public safety and free speech are equally important, and neither one should be valued more highly.

SPEAKER STRATEGIES

Unlike the 1NC in team policy debate, the Negative Constructive in Lincoln-Douglas debate is really two speeches in one. The NC is a combination of the speaker's constructive (pre-written) and first rebuttal (unscripted). He should treat this speech as such: two separate mini-speeches, neither one long constructive nor one long rebuttal.

The negative speaker doesn't need to defeat every point of the affirmative speaker's case, but he can't get away with demonstrating that just one piece of evidence is weak. His strategy should be to concentrate on defeating one or more large element ("observation") in the affirmative's case. The negative's choices are:

1. **Definitions:** The affirmative's definitions are too broad or nebulous to support healthy debate. More precise definitions mean the affirmative's arguments fall outside the resolution.
2. **Value:** The affirmative's value is NOT the one we should hold most highly. The negative can provide an alternative value and argue for its supremacy.
3. **Criterion:** The negative can accept the affirmative's value but argue that we need to use different criterion to measure it. Using the alternative criterion the negative proposes, the affirmative case is not upholding her own value.
4. **Contentions:** The affirmative's contentions do not correspond to the moral claim she is making. Her case lacks sufficient evidence or logical connections to make that claim.

The Rebuttals: Bringing It Home

As in team policy debate, a persuasive rebuttal in Lincoln-Douglas debate begins with good research before the debate. Preparation leaves you with plenty of enthusiasm for your points. A rebuttal is your chance to demonstrate that you understand the opposing points, that you really listened and thought about what has been said, but it wasn't enough. You can still easily refute the arguments.

A beginning debater often does well through the constructive speeches and cross-examinations, only to become exhausted just when it is time to quickly prepare a rebuttal from notes taken. Having fresh evidence or analogies will reinvigorate you and the judges. The extra evidence will help you to think on your feet. Your rebuttal will allude to all the previous good points but will seem fresh, rather than rehashed.

Think about a rebuttal in terms of ancient architecture. Poorly braced roofs, and later the height of cathedrals and castles, created enormous outward pressure on the building materials. So architects added buttresses, sloping support structures that diffused the pressure on the walls. Likewise, while your rebuttal should address the other speaker's case, its most important purpose is to shore up your constructive arguments against the pressure the other speaker has applied.

The rebuttal should consider these three points of attitude:

1. You're grateful that the speakers and judges have come together for the good of debating values.
2. Your opponent has presented specific claims (even if he did it poorly).
3. Your points demonstrate the flaws in his logic and better uphold an important value.

Therefore,

1. you still open and conclude your rebuttal with introductions and thanks,
2. briefly restate your opponent's points, and then
3. spend the majority of your time on your best argument, rebuilding your case and leaving a strong impression on the judge.

SPEAKER STRATEGIES

Imagine the judge's perspective as you assess what you need to do in your last speeches to persuade the judge of your argument.

Is it a…	In other words…	Then why not…?
Disagreement based on FACTS or LOGIC (*logos*)?	"If the judge KNEW this were true, he would understand why my claim is stronger."	Provide an example.
	"If the judge UNDERSTOOD this argument, she would support my claim."	Explain your argument or logic.
Disagreement based on CREDIBILITY (*ethos*)?	"If the judge ACCEPTED my value, he would understand why my claim is stronger."	Share a quotation from a reputable source.
Disagreement based on EMOTION (*pathos*)?	"If the judge FELT the significance of this, she would understand why my claim is stronger."	Tell a story.

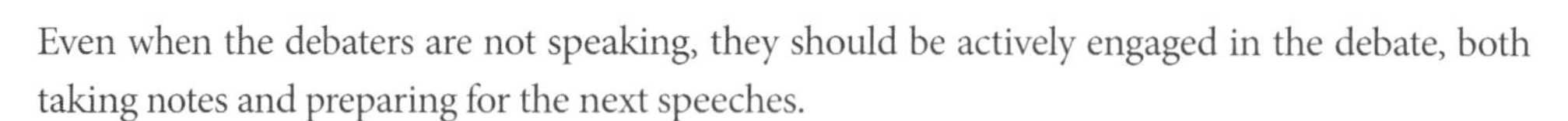

Even when the debaters are not speaking, they should be actively engaged in the debate, both taking notes and preparing for the next speeches.

THE BASICS OF LINCOLN-DOUGLAS DEBATE

The Debater's Role While Listening

Taking Notes with a Flow Chart

Flow-charting is a verb to debaters just like it is to computer programmers and project managers. Flow-charting is the art of making very brief notes in organized columns to ensure both debaters are tracking each other in a debate. There are a few different versions. It's okay to teach one form, but debaters will eventually morph the form to the way they think. New debaters often get so caught up in listening to the debate that they forget to take notes and then forget arguments later.

It is the sign of a seasoned intellect to be able to listen, think, and write all at the same time. Flow-charting hones this skill. Debate has many benefits for students, not the least of which is note-taking practice. Students who wish to practice this outside of debate can practice by taking notes to their pastor's sermon each week. They should try to identify the thesis and the strongest and weakest points used in its defense.

During the debate, students usually use long legal pads to "flow" the round. They divide the pad into a number of columns with a ruled line. The first column lists the particulars of debate that a team is listening for: definitions, value, criterion, and contentions. Each subsequent column is a space for notes from each speech (AC, NC, 1AR, etc.). Some use symbols to keep notes, others write single words, most mix mediums.

Some students include a column for cross-examination and some just keep a sticky pad for cross-examination questions. Students can also put sticky notes into their own speeches so they remember new ideas to argue as they are listening. Others fold up the bottom of the page to form matching columns that can be used to write questions. No matter how you do it, ideally by the end of the debate, an outsider should be able to follow each line of argument across the chart, left to right, from beginning to end.

See the section in Team Policy Debate for examples (pp. 37—38).

Preparing for Upcoming Speeches

AFFIRMATIVE CONSTRUCTIVE (AC)

1. Negative listens well, makes a flow chart, and writes clarifying questions.

CROSS-EXAMINATION OF AC BY N

1. Both stand in front.

PREP TIME*

1. Affirmative notes flaws to overcome and begins to pull evidence from file box to refute possible problems or shore up evidence given.
2. Negative reviews his pre-written case and quickly prepares arguments (using logic, quotations, or anecdotes) to counter the affirmative's contentions.

NEGATIVE CONSTRUCTIVE (NC)

1. Affirmative listens well, takes notes on a flow chart, and writes clarifying questions.

CROSS-EXAMINATION OF NC BY A

1. Both stand in front.

PREP TIME*

1. Affirmative outlines her points in response, using logic, quotations, or anecdotes.

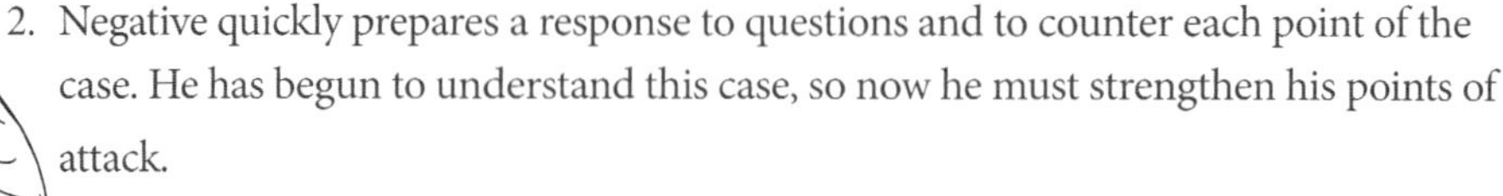

2. Negative quickly prepares a response to questions and to counter each point of the case. He has begun to understand this case, so now he must strengthen his points of attack.

FIRST AFFIRMATIVE REBUTTAL (1AR)

1. Negative listens well and inserts notes into his speech that counter what he is listening to. He pays particular attention to whether the affirmative speaker fails to respond to (drops) an argument.

PREP TIME*

1. Affirmative begins to make notes for final rebuttal.
2. Negative highlights his strongest arguments and makes notes for his closing appeal.

NEGATIVE REBUTTAL (NR)

1. Affirmative listens well and adds notes to flow chart to prepare for final rebuttal.

PREP TIME*

1. Affirmative highlights strongest arguments and makes notes for her closing appeal.

SECOND AFFIRMATIVE REBUTTAL (2AR)

1. Negative listens; speakers shake hands when finished!

*If the speakers choose not to use prep time, or if the speaker has run out by this point, skip this step.

THE BASICS OF LINCOLN-DOUGLAS DEBATE

The Debater's Role While Researching

Now that we've covered what happens during the debate, let's talk about what happens before the debate. Research is a skill that takes time to develop. Be patient, and do not expect in-depth knowledge of the resolution the first time around. To prepare for the affirmative role, debaters should write out their entire case in detail: the constructive argument, possible cross-examination questions and answers, and both rebuttals, gathering fresh anecdotes and quotations for each speech.

In Lincoln-Douglas debate, debaters do write a constructive case for the negative side of the resolution, although they must also address the specific points (contentions) made by the affirmative speaker. Most Lincoln-Douglas cases revolve around competing values—utility vs. beauty, safety vs. freedom, individuals vs. society—that have been around for centuries. Thus, debaters should know a few arguments very well and, when it comes up in the affirmative's constructive, make that the point of attack. Understanding basic principles will make the job easier.

TAG: Cats live completely indoors.

QUOTE: "Cats don't need to be walked outside and would most likely lie down and refuse to budge anyway."

SOURCE: Cato Sockscrates, Professor of Feline Philosophy at School of Athens, "Cat Autonomy." The Complete Philosophy of Cats. Athens: Agora Press, 429 BC. Print.

SUMMARY: Cats can fulfill all of their needs indoors, eliminating the need to go outside to be walked or do

Both speakers should be prepared to present either position, negative or affirmative. This guarantees that they understand both sides of the argument.

As debaters research, they should make notecards or print out quotations that make good points both for and against the resolution. From these cards will come constructive speeches, cross-examination questions, and rebuttals.

GATHERING EVIDENCE

When you begin to research, start general rather than researching a particular side of an argument. This will help you to avoid biased evidence. Lincoln-Douglas has one notable difference from team policy debate when it comes to evidence. Whereas in team policy debate evidence is expected to be current, Lincoln-Douglas debaters may draw from the history of ideas: characters from classic literature, philosophers, or historical leaders. That being said, recent examples are still helpful.

You're looking for quotations, statistics, and examples that will help you make your case. Good places to start are newspaper articles, published collections of quotations, Supreme Court cases, and historical documents like the U.S. Constitution. From these cards and documents will come cross-examination questions, unscripted speeches, and rebuttals.

When you print and file this evidence for future use, be sure to include:

1. The point the quotation or statistic proves (often called a "tagline")

2. The actual quotation or statistic
3. Information about the source and its credentials (date, sponsor, author, title)
4. A longer explanation in your own words explaining the relevance of quote

If the quotation is really good, it can serve as the explanation also. But some debate resolutions are complicated, so you'll need to use your own words to explain a point to the audience. This takes the most time, but it is also the most effective way to engage the judges because it demonstrates that you really understand your case and aren't just reading it.

For example:

> Tagline: Avoiding risks is a better use of time and effort.
>
> > Quote: "A stitch in time saves nine."
> > Source: Thomas Fuller
>
> Summary: If we fix the button before it falls off and rolls away, we save the time finding the button or going to the store to buy another. The lesson? Taking precautions is more prudent than making repairs.

As you research your case, find two to three pieces of evidence (can be anecdotes, quotations, or logical proofs) for each point of your case: one piece for your constructive, and one piece for your rebuttal(s). This is an easy way for a beginner to be ready with lots of evidence.

You should also find two pieces of evidence against your case that reflect the negative of your point. When you are finished with the rough draft of your constructive, look at this evidence again and see if it makes your case look weak. Use it to write a Negative Constructive. Even if you end up presenting the affirmative position, this work will help you think like your opponent.

Write all of these pieces of evidence on notecards or print them on a document and file either by topic or by debate outline.

ASSESSING YOUR EVIDENCE

To ensure that debaters are arguing fairly and honestly, they should assess research carefully. Even though the criterion of timeliness does not apply to Lincoln-Douglas evidence, you should still seek evidence that is as credible and unbiased as possible. The people you quote should have some level of experience or expertise in the matter about which they are speaking. Biases should be carefully explained or acknowledged. Attacking one piece of evidence shouldn't be a substitute for arguing an entire point, but if all of your evidence is one-sided, it might appear that you didn't do your research.

EPILOGUE

Next Steps for Enthusiastic Debaters

Congratulations! You have now completed your basic training in the art of formal debate. If you're interested in learning more, you might be interested in the following resources:

Books

Bortins, Leigh. *The Conversation*. West End, NC: Classical Conversations MultiMedia, 2015.

Jeub, Chris. *Blue Book for Policy Debate*. Monument, CO: Monument Publishing, 2016.

Jeub, Chris. *Red Book for Lincoln-Douglas Debate*. Monument, CO: Monument Publishing, 2016.

Shipe, Christy. *An Introduction to Policy Debate*. 5th ed. Purcellville, VA: HSLDA, 2012.

Organizations

National Christian Forensics and Communications Association (www.ncfca.org)

STOA: Christian Homeschool Speech & Debate (www.stoausa.org)

National Speech & Debate Association (www.speechanddebate.org)

American Forensic Association (www.americanforensics.org)

Cross Examination Debate Association (www.cedadebate.org)

National Educational Debate Association (www.neda.us)

National Parliamentary Debate Association (www.parlidebate.org)

APPENDIX 1

What to Expect on the DVD

This book is accompanied by a two-disc DVD set that provides humorous and serious examples of the forms we have discussed.

DISC 1: TEAM POLICY DEBATE

"The Singing of Christmas Carols Should Be Banned before Thanksgiving."

-with commentary

"The United States Federal Government Should Reform Its Policy to Protect the Value of the U.S. Dollar."

-with commentary

DISC 2: LINCOLN-DOUGLAS DEBATE

"Dogs Make Better Pets than Cats"

-with commentary

"Reading the Book Is Better than Watching the Movie"

-with commentary

BLOOPERS

CREDITS

What to Expect

1. Whereas a real debate would consist of a mix of scripted and unscripted speeches, on these DVDs you will see student actors reading scripted speeches in order to clearly demonstrate the form of each debate.
2. As we worked on this book and the accompanying videos, we made a conscious choice to use silly examples first so that students could focus on the form. Next, we chose imperfect examples so that students could critique someone else's content before developing their own. If the content were perfect, there would be little to discuss and less to learn. Our goal is for you to walk away thinking, "I could do that!" and brimming with ideas for how to improve the content shown.

3. Throughout the debates, green chalkboard pop-ups will point out examples of things done well. Black chalkboard pop-ups will point out areas for improvement.

4. The silly debates come complete with a sample flow chart highlighting each portion of the speech as the debaters complete it. The serious debates omit this feature so you can practice taking notes and following an outline at home.

5. Each debate is also available with judges' audio commentary from two experienced parents and tutors, who will share with you what a coach or judge might look for in assessing each debate.

6. Speeches have been abbreviated for the purposes of this video, and prep time is not shown.

APPENDIX 2

Games

A FEAST AMONG FELLOWS

This activity should take place over a meal, if possible, to cultivate a sense of hospitality and generosity among the participants.

You will need:

- At least four people (and preferably eight to ten)
- A bowl for holding topics
- Slips of paper for writing topics
- A timer or stopwatch

Divide the participants into small groups—no more than four or five people in each. A mix of adults and students in each group is ideal. Ask each participant to submit topics for discussion, ranging from controversial issues such as political parties to philosophical ideas such as whether color or music is more important. The facilitator can help guide participants toward topics that will be appropriate to their maturity level and and their degree of comfort with one another.

The facilitator should pull a topic at random and set the timer for fifteen minutes. At the fifteen-minute mark, the timer goes off, and everyone must immediately stop the discussion. The moderator chooses another topic, and discussion begins for another fifteen minutes. This game will make an hour speed by!

ARISTOTELIAN RHETORIC

Originally published in *The Conversation* by Leigh Bortins.

This game practices Aristotle's three ways of convincing an audience: *logos*, *ethos*, and *pathos*.

You will need:

- Two boxes, bowls, hats, or other containers
- At least three people
- A timer or stopwatch
- A set of notecards numbered 1–5 for each player OR enough erasable surfaces for each player to score the other speakers.

In the first container, place slips of paper each saying "emotion" (*pathos*), "reason/logic" (*logos*), and "authority" (*ethos*). In the second container, place slips of paper saying ridiculous things, which the speaker will have to try to convince the audience are true. Some examples are: "All trees can walk at night," "Time travel has secretly brought dinosaurs to our time, and they will soon take over," and "If you run fast enough you can fly."

To play, one person selects a piece of paper from each container. The first will tell her how she has to convince her audience: either by appealing to the audience's emotions (*pathos*), their reason (*logos*), or to her own or someone else's qualifications as a trusted authority (*ethos*). From the second container, the person will select her topic. She then has two minutes to attempt to convince her audience.

After the two-minute speech is over, each member of the audience will rate how convincing the speech was on a scale of 1–5. You may combine the points or take an average for the speaker's total score. Then it is the next person's turn to speak and the game continues. Compare the scores after each player has had a chance to speak.

SPEECH THIEF

Originally published in *The Conversation* by Leigh Bortins.

"Speech Thief" is loosely based on a BBC Radio 4 comedy called "Just a Minute." This variation was developed by Matt Bianco for use in his Classical Conversations® Challenge IV class.

This game involves thinking on your feet and practicing good rhetorical skills in a friendly but competitive environment.

You will need:

- At least two people
- A book or other source of topics

Choose a topic. The first person (person A) reads a passage from a book. If you don't have a book handy, you can just pick a topic.

The second person (person B) has to talk for one minute about that passage or topic. Person B must stay on topic and do none of the following: repeat himself, pause, say "um," or say "like" unless it is being used to form a comparison.

If he does any of these things, person A may challenge him. If the challenge is successful (the speaker did say "um," for example), person A has the opportunity to finish out the time remaining on the minute.

If person B (the original speaker) completes the entire minute without being challenged, he receives three points. If person A (the thief) challenges him and finishes the minute successfully, she receives one point, and person B (the original speaker) receives only one point. The next round begins with the roles reversed.

Playing with more than two people works the same way. The only difference is that whoever stops the speaker gets to complete the minute. Any one speech can be "stolen" as many times as there are mistakes. Even if the last person says only one word, she will still get the point for completing the minute.

After the student finishes speaking, other students can point out factual inaccuracies. If a student can identify an actual inaccuracy and provide the correct information, he gets one point. Students can earn as many points as there are factual inaccuracies in the speech.

PUT THE ELEMENTS IN ORDER

Write each element of a debate round (1AC, CX of 1AC, 1NC...2AR) on individual note cards. Create two sets. Divide students into two groups and give one set of cards, shuffled, to each group. Groups then race to get the note cards in the right order. The class verifies the order. Alternately, students can work together and race the clock. Do this several times to give all students a chance to participate and practice.

THE QUESTION

Purpose: To help cross-examination skills by training students to think of questions quickly.

Students should sit in a circle. The first person asks the person on their right a question. Rather than answering the question, that person must ask the person on THEIR right a new question. Players cannot reuse questions that have already been asked. If you hesitate, repeat a question, or answer the question, you are out. (Two debate leaders or volunteers may wish to demonstrate first.) Keep going around the circle until only one player is left.

Player 1 to Player 2: "What is your favorite color?"

Player 2 to Player 3: "Is it cold today?"

Player 3: "Yes." (Player 3 is out)

FOUR CORNERS

On strips of paper, write out 10-20 sentences, each demonstrating an argument based on one of the four stock issues: significance, inherency, topicality, and solvency.

These statements may refer to a topic you are using in class, or to a variety of imaginary topics. The goal is to include key words that give students a hint about which stock issue is at stake. (Do not name the stock issue explicitly. See next page for examples.)

Station volunteers in the four corners of the room, and assign one of the stock issues to each of them.

Put the strips on a table and have the students pick one up at a time and figure out which stock issue it references. The students will take the stock issue slip to its corresponding stock issue corner. The volunteer in that corner will look it over (or ask the student to read the slip aloud) and tell the student if he or she picked the correct stock issue. If students incorrectly identify the stock issue, the volunteers can give hints to help them find the correct location.

Students can compete in teams or against the clock to correctly place all of the statements. A coach or the students themselves can also create more statements to expand the game.

STOCK ISSUE STATEMENTS

Significance (clue words: enormous, important, all, substantial)

All Americans have been affected by high fuel costs.

Immigration is one of the largest issues facing our generation.

International sanctions cause American companies to lose substantial revenue.

Inherency (clue words: already, built-in, continue, cause)

The immigration policy is already being reformed by Congress.

Grades will continue to drop if the status quo remains the same.

Alternatives to oil are already being developed in the private sector.

Topicality (clue words: define, resolution, bounds, exclude)

The affirmative does not follow the resolution because they are talking about state policy, not federal policy.

A sloop is a small warship with guns on only one deck.

The affirmative is not meeting his definition of constructive engagement.

Solvency (clue words: fix, improve, plan, better)

This plan will help lower the crime rate.

Once we make this change, both countries' economies will improve.

The best way to fix our immigration policy is to adopt this plan.

Appendix 3: Tool for Assessing Debate

TEAM POLICY	INVENTION Assess **evidence** using the CPR method (credible, published, and—in team policy only—recent)	LINCOLN-DOUGLAS
1A		A
2A		
1N		N
2N		
	ARRANGEMENT Assess **refutation** by determining whether the speaker (1) rebuilt his or her case, and (2) tore down his opponent's case, responding directly to arguments rather than simply presenting contrary quotations.	
1A		A
2A		
1N		N
2N		
	ELOCUTION Assess the speaker's use of *pathos, logos,* and *ethos* in persuasion.	
1A		A
2A		
1N		N
2N		
	MEMORY Assess **cross-examination** using the ABCs (accurate, brief, careful) for answering questions and ACE (ask questions, clarify arguments, expose weaknesses) for asking questions.	
1A		A
2A		
1N		N
2N		
	DELIVERY Assess eye contact, posture, volume, enunciation, and any distracting tendencies (shuffling papers, rocking podium) in the speaker's **delivery**.	
1A		A
2A		
1N		N
2N		

APPENDIX 4

Sample Team Policy Debate Script

FIRST AFFIRMATIVE CONSTRUCTIVE SPEECH

1AC Are the judges ready? Is the timer ready? Negative team?

Good morning. *(Timer begins clock.)* My partner, [partner's name], and I, [your name], are for the resolution: The singing of Christmas carols should be banned before Thanksgiving.

Quote: "Christmas carols are for Christmas time only, if they must be sung at all," said Ebenezer Scrooge.

Observation 1: Definitions

Singing: making a raucous nose whether or not people want to hear it
SOURCE: InSupportOfEars.com

Christmas carols: a song whose lyrics are on the theme of Christmas
SOURCE: The Christmas Dictionary

Banned: prohibited forbidden
SOURCE: Dictionary.com

Thanksgiving:aA holiday held on the fourth Thursday of November
SOURCE: The U.S. Code

Observation 2: Harms

Harm A: People with a sensible view of Christmas carols are afraid to go out in public in November.

Quote: "I have to carry earmuffs to ward off unwanted attacks of 'Jingle Bells' in the department stores," shouted Grandmother Houser.
SOURCE: PetPeevesAnonymous, January 2014

Summary: Christmas-carol singing is dangerous and discriminatory.

Harm B: Christmas carol lyrics only make sense in December.

Quote: "If you look outside in July, there is no snow for sleigh rides and snowmen," explained the National Weather Service.
SOURCE: NWS Howler, June 2015

Summary: Christmas carols should be sung only when they make sense.

Observation 3: The Plan

Mandate: People who sing Christmas carols before Thanksgiving will be fined $50.

Agency: The executive branch of the United States government

Enforcement: Mall cops

Funding: The administrative and enforcement costs will be covered by the fines.

Observation 4: Advantages

Advantage A: All people will be able to shop in peace.

Summary: They will no longer have to hide from unwanted Christmas carols before Thanksgiving.

Advantage B: Christmas carols will no longer be confusing.

Summary: People will be able to relate to the winter scenes described in carols.

In Conclusion:

Quote: "Christmas is in December, not September, and we should treat it appropriately," said Jack Frost.

Therefore, my partner, [partner's name], and I urge the judges to vote for the resolution. Thank you. I am now ready for cross-examination.

SECOND NEGATIVE CROSS-EXAMINATION OF FIRST AFFIRMATIVE

CX of 1AC by 2N

CX: Good morning.

1A: Good morning.

CX: Is the timer ready?

(Timer begins clock)

May I have a copy of your 1AC?

1A: My partner will be happy to pass a copy to your partner.

CX: Thank you. Could you describe the biases of InSupportOfEars.com?

1A: In a fair way, they explain the effect of everyday choices on innocent ears.

*CX:*Do you propose to ban rap and jazz as well?

*1A:*No. Our resolution today is specifically about Christmas carols.

CX: What is the current job of mall cops?

1A: They make sure the mall is a good environment for everyone.

CX: Thank you. I have no further questions.

FIRST NEGATIVE CONSTRUCTIVE SPEECH

1NC: Are the judges ready? Timer? Affirmative team?

Good morning. *(Timer begins clock.)* My partner, [partner's name], and I, [your name], stand against the resolution: The singing of Christmas carols should be banned before Thanksgiving.

Quote: "The best way to spread Christmas cheer is singing loud for all to hear," said Buddy the Elf, from the movie Elf.

Observation 1: Definitions

My partner and I accept the affirmative team's definitions except for "singing." This definition is biased and makes singing sound like a bad thing. We propose instead:

Singing: making beautiful music that makes people happy.

SOURCE: SingersUnited.com.

1N

Observation 2: Harms

Harm A: The affirmative team says people with a sensible view of Christmas carols are afraid to go out in public in November, BUT…

Quote: "Traffic was up 50% in November last year," according to the The Ghost of Christmas Past.

SOURCE: Holiday Traffic Coalition, November 2014.

Summary: The number of people staying home out of fear cannot be significant.

Harm B: The affirmative team says Christmas carol lyrics only make sense in December, BUT…

Quote: "Once I had my first Christmas, I understood Christmas carols. Period. It's not like I forget snow in January" says Baby New Year.

SOURCE: RightsForBabies, October 2015.

Summary: Christmas carols make sense to anyone who has been alive in December at least once. This is a tiny problem.

Observation 3: The Plan

The affirmative team's plan will not work. We are happy with the status quo.

Enforcement: Mall cops do not have jurisdiction in grocery stores and other places where Christmas carols are played. Plus, they are already overworked.

Observation 4: Advantages

Advantage A: The affirmative team says all people will be able to shop in peace, BUT...

Quote: "I hate jazz music, but somehow I still manage to ride in elevators," said Mildred Millionaire.

SOURCE: Complainers Anonymous, March 2012.

Summary: Unless you ban all music from malls, someone will be unhappy.

Advantage B: The affirmative team says Christmas carols will no longer be confusing, BUT....

Quote: "Every year, there are more and more mumblers who don't know the words to Christmas carols. It's a monstrosity!" said Wenceslaus I, Duke of Bohemia

SOURCE: North Pole Carol Patrol, November 2014.

Summary: People will have only a month to learn Christmas carols, so they will be MORE confusing, not less. A ban doesn't fix anything.

In Conclusion:

Quote: "I will honor Christmas in my heart, and try to keep it all the year," said Charles Dickens.

Therefore, my partner, [partner's name], and I urge the judges to vote against the resolution. Thank you. I am now ready for cross-examination.

FIRST AFFIRMATIVE CROSS-EXAMINATION OF FIRST NEGATIVE

CX: Good morning.

1N: Good morning.

CX: Is the timer ready?

(Timer begins clock)

Can you tell me the mission of SingersUnited.com?

1N: It's the online meet-up site for carolers.

CX: Did you provide any evidence that mall cops are overworked?

1N: My partner will be glad to provide some.

CX: Thank you. I have no further questions.

SECOND AFFIRMATIVE CONSTRUCTIVE SPEECH

2A: Are the judges ready? Timer? Negative team?

Good morning. *(Timer begins clock)* My partner, [partner's name], and I, [your name], are for the resolution: The singing of Christmas Carols should be banned before Thanksgiving.

Quote: "Christmas is only special if we celebrate it at Christmas time," declared Frosty the Snowman.

Observation 1: Definitions

We do not accept the negative team's alternative definition. Singers United obviously has something to gain from there being more singing.

The affirmative team is pleased that the negative has accepted our other definitions.

Observation 2: Harms

Harm A: People with a sensible view of Christmas carols are afraid to go out in public in November.

Quote: "Last week, I saw three cases of people who had jumped into the mall fountain to avoid 'Have Yourself a Merry Little Christmas,'" said Dr. Waterlog.
SOURCE: Association for Doctors Near Shopping Malls, 2015.

Summary: People who want Christmas to be special should not have to suffer.

Harm B: Christmas carol lyrics only make sense in December.

Quote: "Have you ever tried to explain 'Good King Wenceslas' to a swimming pool full of toddlers?" asked Betty Babysitter.
SOURCE: Against Christmas In July, Vol. 2, 2013.

Summary: Snow does not lay round about in July.

Observation 3: The Plan

Let me restate our plan:

Mandate: People who sing Christmas carols before Thanksgiving will be fined $50.

Agency: The executive branch of the United States government

Enforcement: Mall cops

Funding: The administrative and enforcement costs will be covered by the fines.

Observation 4: Advantages

Advantage A: All people will be able to shop in peace.

Summary: Shoppers will not be continuously accosted by the "Twelve Days of Christmas."

Advantage B: Christmas carols will no longer be confusing.

Summary: Carolers will have context for the words they are singing.

In Conclusion:

Quote: "Leave the yuletide carols until it's time for yule logs. That's the only proper thing to do," said the Yule Log Manufacturers of America.

Therefore, my partner, [partner's name], and I urge the judges to vote for the resolution. Thank you. I am now ready for cross-examination.

FIRST NEGATIVE CROSS-EXAMINATION OF SECOND AFFIRMATIVE

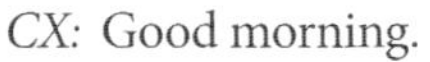

CX: Good morning.

1N: Good morning.

CX: Is the timer ready?

(Timer begins clock)

Could you explain how Dr. Waterlog is an authority on Christmas carols?

1N: He is a senior physician in the hospital next door to one of the biggest malls in the state, so he knows what endangers shoppers.

CX: Has Betty Babysitter ever explained anything successfully to a pool full of toddlers?

1N: No, but Christmas carols are particularly difficult for her.

CX: How did you arrive at $50 for a fine?

1N CX 2A

1N: It is in proportion to the seriousness of the crime.

CX: So is $50 a fine for a small problem or a large one?

1N: It is a small problem that is becoming large.

CX: Thank you. I have no further questions.

SECOND NEGATIVE CONSTRUCTIVE SPEECH

2N: Are the judges ready? Timer? Affirmative team?

Good morning. *(Timer begins clock)* My partner, [partner's name], and I, [your name], stand against the resolution: The singing of Christmas Carols should be banned before Thanksgiving.

Quote: "Happiness multiplied by happiness equals happiness squared," said the Math Teachers Association.

Observation 1: Definitions

The negative team accepts the affirmative definitions except for "singing." We urge the judges to adopt our dictionary form of the word "singing" as a more descriptive, less divisive definition.

Observation 2: Harms

Harm A: The affirmative team says people with a sensible view of Christmas carols are afraid to go out in public in November, BUT...

Quote: "Last year, over two thousand people were injured trying to climb over other patrons to escape the opera," said the Coalition Against Microphones for Sopranos.
SOURCE: CAMS Newsletter, 2015

Summary: The affirmative team is ignoring the people who dislike other kinds of music. They are far more numerous.

Harm B: The affirmative team says Christmas carol lyrics only make sense in December, BUT...

Quote: "It's not about making sense, it's about freedom of expression," said Dr. C. Flat, of the law firm Flat, Sharp, and Natural.
SOURCE: White Paper 999, October 2012

Summary: People having a right to sing is more important than any minor confusion that may occur.

Observation 3: The Plan

Mandate: People who sing Christmas carols before Thanksgiving will be fined $50. This is a small fine, and as the affirmative team admitted in cross-examination, it answers a small problem.

Enforcement: Mall cops are already overworked.

Quote: "I am on my feet all day," said the Blogging Mall Cop, a local celebrity.

We urge the judges to maintain the status quo.

Observation 4: Advantages

Advantage A: The affirmative team says all people will be able to shop in peace, BUT...

Summary: People who hate classical music never have the opportunity to shop in peace. Why should Christmas haters receive special treatment?

Advantage B: The affirmative team says Christmas carols will no longer be confusing, BUT...

Summary: The affirmative team's examples deal with babies, who also find washing machines and object permanence confusing. This is not a real problem.

In Conclusion:

Quote: "Christmas carols are about peace on earth. We should be singing them more, not less," said The Ghost of Christmas Present.

Therefore, my partner, [partner's name], and I urge the judges to maintain the status quo. Thank you. I am now ready for cross-examination.

2N

SECOND AFFIRMATIVE CROSS-EXAMINATION OF SECOND NEGATIVE

CX: Good morning.

2N: Good morning.

CX: Is the timer ready?

(Timer begins clock)

What is the reason you do not accept the affirmative's definition for singing?

2N: We disagree with your emotional appeal to insignificant incidents.

CX: When did the Blogging Mall Cop find time to become famous, if he was overworked?

2N: He has not shared that information with fans.

CX: Thank you. I have no further questions.

FIRST NEGATIVE REBUTTAL

1NR: Are the judges ready? Timer? Affirmative team?

Good morning. *(Timer begins clock)* My partner, [partner's name], and I, [your name], are against the resolution: The singing of Christmas Carols should be banned before Thanksgiving.

Observation 1: Definitions

The negative team stands with our definition on singing. It better describes the act of singing without being emotional. We urge the judges to adopt our dictionary definition from SingersUnited.com.

Observation 2: Harms

Christmas carols are no more troublesome than any other kind of music. Citizens should have the right to sing what they want. Let's put the rare problem in its proper perspective.

Observation 3: Plan

Again, the negative team urges the judges to reject the need for any plan that reduces or eliminates the singing of Christmas carols all year round.

Mall cops are already overworked and do not need any additional responsibilities.

Observation 4: Advantages

The affirmative team's plan will not solve the minor problems they have identified. People will occasionally be irritated by Christmas music, but occasional harm does not necessitate complete banning.

Therefore, my partner, [partner's name], and I urge the judges to maintain the status quo. Thank you.

FIRST AFFIRMATIVE REBUTTAL

1AR: Are the judges ready? Timer? Negative team?

Good morning. *(Timer begins clock)* My partner, [partner's name], and I, [your name], are for the resolution: The singing of Christmas Carols should be banned before Thanksgiving.

Quote: "Let us anticipate Christmas for once, I beg you," said the Ghost of Christmas Yet to Come.

Observation 1: Definitions

Our disagreement on the definition for singing explains why we are having this debate. Those who have been injured by its irresponsible use are concerned with the safety of others. Those who like to sing selfishly overlook its misuse.

Observation 2: Harms

Harm A: People with a sensible view of Christmas carols are afraid to go out in public in November. Just because they are not the only ones suffering from obnoxious sounds does not mean we should abandon this important group of sensible people.

Harm B: Christmas carol lyrics only make sense in December. Without a real-world reference, people will not understand what they mean.

Observation 3: Plan

Our plan will work. People who sing Christmas carols before Thanksgiving will be fined $50.

Mall cops are fully capable of taking on the responsibility of enforcement.

Observation 4: Advantages

If we ban Christmas carols before Thanksgiving, all people will be able to shop in peace, and Christmas carols will no longer be confusing.

In Conclusion:

Quote: "Christmas carols are like salt—in an open wound. Less is more," said Ebenezer Scrooge.

Therefore, my partner, [partner's name], and I urge the judges to vote for the resolution. Thank you.

1 AR

SECOND NEGATIVE REBUTTAL

2NR: Are the judges ready? Timer? Affirmative team?

Good morning. *(Timer begins clock)* My partner, [partner's name], and I, [your name], are against the resolution: The singing of Christmas Carols should be banned before Thanksgiving.

Observation 1: Definitions

The negative team stands with our definition of singing.

It is much less emotionally charged.

The affirmative's case is as emotionally charged as its definition.

We urge the judges to adopt our dictionary form of the definition.

Observation 2: Harms

There are no harms inherent to singing Christmas carols at any time of year. There is more harm in overworking already busy mall cops by making them patrol grocery stores. Furthermore, the affirmative team has not responded to our challenge about the freedom of expression, a fundamental right.

Observation 3: Plan

Please reject the emotional arguments of a few people who dislike Christmas carols. The proposed ban is not a logical reaction to a few incidents. If irritating noises formed law, we would ban windshield wipers, chalkboards, and Styrofoam. Let's be reasonable and continue to celebrate Christmas carols.

Observation 4: Advantages

Christmas carols bring joy to the people who sing them, whether in December or July. Any problems they may cause are insignificant in comparison.

> Quote: "No one can sing, 'Ho ho ho' with a frown on his face," said Saint Nicholas.

Therefore, my partner, [partner's name], and I urge the judges to maintain the status quo. Thank you.

SECOND AFFIRMATIVE REBUTTAL

2AR: Are the judges ready? Timer? Negative team?

Good morning. *(Timer begins clock)* My partner, [partner's name], and I, [your name], are for the resolution: The singing of Christmas carols should be banned before Thanksgiving.

Quote: "Dashing through the snow is hard to do in the mud," said the Rudolph the Red-Nosed Reindeer.

Observation 1: Definitions

Again, singing should not be a selfish act, and it does not make everyone happy all the time. Therefore, we stand by our definition.

Observation 2: Harms

People with a sensible view of Christmas carols are afraid to go out in public in November. Christmas carols are a unique source of irritation when they are used outside their proper place, where the lyrics make sense.

Observation 3: Plan

So, the affirmative team will stick with our plan. Let me remind you of our key points.

Mandate: People who sing Christmas carols before Thanksgiving will be fined $50.

Agency: The executive branch of the United States government

Enforcement: Mall cops

Funding: The administrative and enforcement costs will be covered by the fines.

Observation 4: Advantages

All people will be able to shop in peace, and when they do sing Christmas carols, they will no longer be confused.

In Conclusion:

Let's heed the advice of Grandmother Houser, Ebenezer Scrooge, and the National Weather Service, and keep Christmas carols in December, where they belong.

Therefore, my partner, [partner's name], and I urge the judges to vote for the resolution. Thank you.

APPENDIX 5

Sample Lincoln-Douglas Debate Script

AFFIRMATIVE CONSTRUCTIVE SPEECH

AC: QUOTE: "A dog teaches a boy fidelity, playfulness, and to turn around three times before lying down."—Clifford, the Big Red Dog

The value of a pet is directly connected to how much companionship or pleasure it provides. The vastly superior intelligence of a dog allows it to learn new skills to continually interact with the owner, whereas a cat will only interact with its owner when it wants to, which is hardly ever.

Thus, I, [your name], agree with Clifford the Big Red Dog and therefore stand for the resolution: "Dogs make better pets than cats."

Definitions

Dog: a hairy domesticated animal that is fond of slobbering
Source: CanidDictionaries.com

Cat: a furry domesticated mammal that is adept at slinking
Source: FelixDictionaries.com

Better: more desirable, satisfactory, or effective
Source: Merriam-Webster.com

Pet: a domestic or tamed animal kept for companionship or pleasure
Source: OxfordDictionaries.com

Value: INTELLIGENCE

Criterion: The ability to learn new skills

Contentions

Contention 1: Dogs know how to protect their owners.

QUOTE: "When there is someone in need, doggie heroes are often the first responders." —I. M. Shaggy; Doctor of Doggie Philosophy

Dogs have an innate sensibility to protect people and instinctively scare off or attack intruders. In an emergency, dogs have been known to call 911, and everyone knows that Lassie saved Timmy from a thousand deaths.

Contention 2: Dogs can be trained to serve their owners.

> QUOTE: "I tried to teach my teenager to bring me the mail, the paper, my slippers, answer the phone, fetch food and water, and greet people at the door, but my dog learned it first." —Pluto, Greek philosopher

Dogs can be trained to perform many useful household services. Behavior modification techniques can enhance the owner-pet relationship while helping the dog become a well-mannered member of the family, maybe even the best-mannered.

Contention 3: Dogs know how to play and interact with their owners.

> QUOTE: "Dogs love to fetch, play tug-of-war, and chase a ball. Their keen doggy skills make them adept at all types of play and interaction with people, but they're lousy at card games." —Snoopy, author of *It's Doggone Pawsible, a Pooch Memoir*

In summary, dogs can interact with their owners and show their affection through a variety of play activities such as fetching, chasing, tugging, and going for walks.

(Conclusion)

Dogs live to please their owners. Whereas a cat is persnickety, often completely ignoring its owner, a dog never turns down an opportunity to engage with its owner and can be trained to protect, serve, and play—clearly showing that "Dogs make better pets than cats."

Therefore, I urge the judges to make the "intelligent" choice and vote for the affirmative! Thank you; I now stand open for cross-examination.

NEGATIVE CROSS-EXAMINATION OF AFFIRMATIVE

CX: Would you say that dogs that scare off intruders or attackers are acting aggressively?

A: Yes, but. . .

CX: Thank you, all I need is a yes or no answer.

Would you say that most families when shopping for a pet are looking for an aggressive animal?

A: No, probably not.

CX: When a dog brings his owner the mail, the paper, or her slippers, isn't it true that they're often covered with disgusting dog slobber?

A: Yes, but the disgusting part is subjective.

CX: Isn't it true that besides bringing their owners the mail, the paper, or slippers, they also bring undesirable things like smelly garbage, a favorite designer shoe, or as the story goes, a student's homework?

A: Yes, there have been cases reported.

CX: In your third contention, (dogs know how to play) isn't it true that dogs have been known to play with things that are not toys, such as Snowball, the family's former pet hamster?

A: Yes, there have been some unfortunate instances.

CX: Thank you, I have no more questions.

NEGATIVE CONSTRUCTIVE SPEECH

(Introduction)

NC: QUOTE: "A cat teaches a boy self-reliance, patience, and how to turn his nose up at a meal." —Ancient Patagonian Proverb

While it is true that dogs interact well with their owners, this can often transform the dog into a needy, neurotic animal that can't be left alone for five minutes without wreaking canine havoc. Cats, however, while also offering human companionship, are far less needy than dogs.

Thus, I, [your name], agree with the wisdom of the ancient proverb and am therefore opposed to the resolution: "Dogs make better pets than cats."

Observation 1: Definitions

I accept all of the affirmative's definitions for this round.

Observation 2: Value

INDEPENDENCE

Observation 2: Criterion

The ability to rely less on human beings for care and well-being

Observation 4: Contentions

Contention 1: Cats are able to clean and maintain themselves.

QUOTE: "The smallest feline is a masterpiece, and any cat will be the first to agree with this." —Leonardo (Leo) da Lionnici, Renaissance artist

QUOTE: "Cats don't stink." —Mittens, author of *Lick This, Don't Lick That*

Cats self-bathe, and because cats constantly clean and groom themselves they do not offend the nasal passages of their owners. Dogs don't have this ability, and without regular bathing by their owners, no one cares how smart they are because of how smelly they are.

Contention 2: Cats can live completely indoors.

QUOTE: "Cats don't need to be walked outside and would most likely lie down and refuse to budge, anyway." —Sockscrates

Cats can fulfill all of their needs indoors, eliminating the need to go outside to be walked or do their business, as well as worries or concerns when the owner is at work or away from home. Most dogs, when they are out, want to be in, and vice versa, and often simultaneously.

Contention 3: Cats don't require basic training.

> QUOTE: "Bring a kitty home as a pet and it's ready to use. Bring a puppy home as a pet and you bring home doggie disaster." —René De Cats, French philosopher

Cats don't require any basic training to be a good pet. Without some basic training, dogs don't make very good pets—they make trouble, and much of their trouble centers around eating disorders and bladder control.

Response to Affirmative Case

(Attack on 1st Affirmative Contention)

In the dog's own words, he is not intelligent enough to know real danger.

> QUOTE: "Once again, my vicious bark has saved my family from the evil doings of the mailman, and I was quite pleased to rid the yard of those dangerous squirrels, but I am especially proud to have cleared those treacherous little girls in uniform away from the front door. Although I did enjoy those boxes of cookies they left behind. —Chewboxes, Film Star (*Star Wars*)

A dog's aggressive nature is often misdirected. Cats don't disturb the peace: they quietly remove themselves when guests or visitors arrive, and they couldn't care less about the mailman, unless he has mail for them.

(Attack on 2nd Affirmative Contention)

> QUOTE: It's true that dogs have been trained to serve their owners; in fact, domestication has left dogs brain-washed! Dogs have been so dumbed-down that all they know is what they've been taught. Dogs have lost their survival skills and would need a cat to guide them in the wild. Dogs run away and don't have the sense to come home; and when left home alone without their owners, dogs do bad things worthy of the doggy hall of shame. It's no coincidence that the dog owner's first words are, "Bad dog! Bad dog!" —Dr. Seuss, director of The Center for Rehabilitation of Domesticated, Dumbed-down Dogs

(Attack on 3rd Affirmative Contention)

I agree with the affirmative that dogs know how to play. What my opponent failed to mention is that dogs are non-discriminating and will play with anything.

> QUOTE:"At first it appeared that Rover and Snowball, the pet hamster, were getting along fine, until the tragedy happened." —Dr. Doolittle, Veterinary Hospital for the Surgical Removal of Stuff from Dog Stomachs

> QUOTE: "We tell them over and over, it's just a stick—there's no need to keep bringing it back, but they just don't seem to understand." —Dr. Dachshund Freud, Pet Psychoanalyst

Training dogs to play and interact with their owners has made dogs so dependent on pleasing their owners that they have become attuned only to human desires and feelings.

> QUOTE: "It's usually more common in pigs, but we see dog cases, too. You can look from dog to man, and from man to dog, and sometimes it's almost impossible to tell which is which." —George Orwell, author of *Animal Farm*

(Conclusion)

Whereas dogs might be smart enough to learn new skills, they lack ability to use those skills in a consistently well-behaved manner and often use those skills to do more harm than good. The independent nature of cats, on the other hand, makes them an ideal pet. They do not require any basic training, and their self-reliance means their owners do not need to do much to care for and maintain them. Therefore, I stand firmly against the resolution "Dogs make better pets than cats."

Thank you; I now stand open for cross-examination.

AFFIRMATIVE CROSS-EXAMINATION OF NEGATIVE

CX: You mentioned in your first contention that cats clean themselves. Would you please explain how they do that?

N: They lick themselves clean.

CX: Nice. And do they ever ingest any fur while they are licking themselves?

N: Yes, they do.

CX: Your second contention stated that cats can live completely indoors. How do they go to the bathroom?

N: They use a litter box.

CX: They use a litter box, and they clean that litter box themselves, do they?

N: No, they do not.

CX: So someone has the happy chore of cleaning that litter box?

N: Yes.

CX: Thank you. Your third contention said that cats don't require any basic training. Would you say that cats are perfectly behaved pets?

N: No, I wouldn't say that they're perfect.

CX: Which animal, then, would you say is easier to train, a cat or a dog?

N: Well, I'm not an expert, but I would say the dog is easier to train.

CX: Thank you, I have no more questions.

FIRST AFFIRMATIVE REBUTTAL

(Response to Negative Case)

Value: I will demonstrate that intelligence, not independence, is the better value when choosing a pet, and I will use the criterion of a dog's ability to learn new skills to uphold my value.

QUOTE: "Dogs have evolved a greater ability in social communication than cats, and that's why they get invited to more parties." —Anonymous.

(Contentions)

Contention 1: The negative's assertion that cats are able to clean and maintain themselves is overstated. While a cat may be able to clean itself, there is a repugnant consequence.

QUOTE: "Pardon me; I'm afraid I have to expel a rather ferocious hairball."—The Cheshire Cat to Alice in *There's Something Not So Wonderful in Wonderland*

QUOTE: "Dog owners only have to clean the outside of their dogs; they don't have to clean up what's inside." —Charles Dickens, author of *Great Expectorations*

Contention 2: The negative also asserted that cats don't need to go outside. Cats can use that most aesthetic of inventions, the litter box.

QUOTE: "I'm just trying to oblige my owners. I can't imagine what they want with it, but since they keep emptying it, I keep filling it." —Hercules, World's Largest Domestic Cat

It doesn't take much imagination to recall the unpleasantness associated with hairballs and litter boxes. But besides being nasty, litter boxes are dangerous!

QUOTE: "Microscopic spores that are spread through insects can come in direct contact with cat feces. Once they infect a human, they cause the disease toxoplasmosis. This disease causes severe birth defects in pregnant women, which is why doctors tell pregnant women that they should never empty litter boxes or otherwise clean up after cats." —Jay Wile, *Exploring Creation through Biology*

This can create a problem in the cat-owning household since every other member of the family will deny having the pooper-scooper gene.

Contention 3: The negative's third contention is that dogs need to be trained. At least dogs can be trained; cats only serve themselves and are not interested in being trained beyond their own needs.

QUOTE: "In ancient times cats were worshiped as gods; they have not forgotten this."—Cleocatra, famous Egyptian historian

(Rebuild Affirmative Case)

In returning to my case, the quality of intelligence in a pet is essential in ensuring the best family pet. The dog's ability to learn new skills demonstrates its ability to learn and adapt to its new family.

1. My opponent claims that a dog is not intelligent enough to know real danger and barks unnecessarily. A dog can be trained not to bark inappropriately, but the real problem here is usually the dog owner, not the dog. Owners often unknowingly reinforce or reward the barking.

   QUOTE: "I'm very excited about this new development in The Master. He seems to be learning to communicate in my language. Every time I bark he shouts at me. I haven't quite learned the vocabulary but it's clear from the volume of his vociferations that he is communicating his approval! This is reward indeed—I can't wait to repeat the behavior to show him I understand!" —Beowoof, Literary hero to the Great Danes

2. The negative claims that dogs have lost their survival skills in the wild. Examples from the historical record would indicate the contrary. To cite just one example, in Episode 248 of Scooby-Doo, Where Are You! Scooby and his friend, Fifi the labradoodle, escape a haunted castle in the Australian outback and cleverly find their way back to Shaggy and the gang.

3. Finally, my opponent has argued that dogs are non-discriminating and will play with things that are not play toys. As I have said before, dogs can be trained to behave appropriately, but man's attempts to discipline a cat have failed miserably.

   QUOTE: "Dogs respond to discipline with abject guilt and remorse, a cat's response to discipline is, 'Bring it!'" —Dr. Dachshund Freud, Pet Psychoanalyst

In conclusion, intelligence in a domestic pet is a value that allows the animal to adapt to its new home and new family. Thank you.

NEGATIVE REBUTTAL

(Response to Affirmative Attacks)

1. The Affirmative has brought up the fact that cats have hairballs, but cats don't have to go to the ER to remove the hairball; cats can quickly, efficiently, and inexpensively remove their own foreign objects.

   QUOTE: "We've only had two dog patients in here today and already we've removed a roll of toilet paper, a Star Wars Lego figure, three socks, and Tweety." —Dr. Doolittle, Veterinary Hospital for the Surgical Removal of Stuff from Dog Stomachs

2. To address the affirmative's attack on the litterbox, I would like to point out that dogs have halitosis, which is worse than toxoplasmosis! Who wants to brush a dog's teeth every day? Toxoplasmosis is rare and can be avoided, but doggy breath is a residing evil.

   QUOTE: "Doggy breath is a common problem; one solution is to pour mouthwash in the toilet." —Willy "Woofy" Wonka, Dr. of Doggy Dentistry

In further defense of cats and the litter box, at least cats bury their business.

   QUOTE: "Dogs don't know when a thing needs to be buried, and I don't mean bones." —Dr.W. Pooh, Doctor of Scatological Studies

3. Finally, dogs are brainwashed; but true to their independent nature, cats have minds of their own. More than any other animal on the planet, "Dogs are tuned in to the 'human radio frequency.' Indeed, humans may be the only station dogs listen to. Cats, on the other hand, can tune in if they want to. Cats, as any owner knows, are highly intelligent beings. But to science, their minds may forever be a black box." – Dr. Dachshund Freud, Pet Psychoanalyst

(Make Final Negative Case)

In closing, history supports the value of the independent cat: Leonardo da Vinci recognized the cat as the masterpiece of God, and the Egyptians valued cats so highly that they worshiped them. It was the Cheshire Cat that had to help Alice, not vice versa, and compared to Garfield, Odie the dog was the village idiot. We find further support in classic literature. Charles Dickens, author of *A Tale of Two Kitties*, has asked, "What greater gift than the love of an undemanding cat?"

(Show Weaknesses of Affirmative Case)

Independence is the quality that provides pet owners with the ideal pet. You get all of the affection without the noise, maintenance, disruption, and disaster.

The affirmative case has failed to show how dogs are able to clean and maintain themselves. A dog's idea of bathing itself is to go outside and roll on its back on a dung heap.

The affirmative's case has also failed to account for a dog's incessant need to go outside, since really a dog is nothing more than a fur-covered kidney that barks. Before dogs, "piddle" was not a word you would find in the dictionary.

The affirmative's case has failed to counter our argument that dogs will play with anything, as evidenced by our examples of Snowball and Tweety, may they rest in peace.

Finally, let us look at my opponent's claim that dogs can be trained in new skills to protect and serve their owners. If someone wants service, then he should get a copy of the Yellow Pages. The cat does not offer services. The cat offers itself. As Founding Father Tomcat Jefferson put it, "Cats were put into the world to disprove the DOGma that all things were created to serve man." The plain truth is that dogs are needy, brain-washed, undisciplined animals that require more of their owners than they give in return.

QUOTE: "A cat will never bring the police to your door by his ritual 2 A.M. barking. He won't attack the mailman or terrify the Girl Scouts, and he won't eat the drapes, although he may climb the drapes, but this is just to see if the curtain rods have been mounted properly." —Ellis Peters, author of *A Morbid Taste for Milkbones*

(Summarize Negative Case)

In summary, the negative case has proven that independence is the better value when choosing a pet. Cats can clean and maintain themselves, they need never go outdoors, and they don't require basic training to achieve harmony and a minimum of order in the home.

It is for these reasons that I stand firmly resolved that cats make better pets than dogs and I urge the judge to award a negative ballot at the end of today's round.

SECOND AFFIRMATIVE REBUTTAL

(Response to Negative Rebuttal)

Families searching for a pet want interaction, not a machine. If I want something that is self-cleaning and ignores me, then I can buy a new oven. The negative case wants us to believe that the autonomy of a cat is what brings satisfaction to its owner, but I contend that the deep interaction of a dog with its owner provides pure joy and true satisfaction. Families do not seek a pet in order to have something to avoid; families seek a pet in order to have new member of the family—one that is more interested in rolling over than roll-over minutes.

(Summarize Case)

The negative case would have us believe that when a family looks for a pet they want something that stays clean, stays indoors, and doesn't need basic training. I contend that that family does not want a pet. What that family wants is Grandma.

The affirmative has clearly shown the importance of intelligence and how this value makes a dog a better companion than an aloof, snooty, and disinterested cat. A quick comparison will cement the argument. Dogs can be trained to protect their owners; cats cannot, but they will at least be clean at their owner's funeral. Dogs can be taught to fetch things for their owners; cats, which according to the negative case, can live forever indoors, cannot be bothered to fetch up anything other than a hairball. And finally, dogs can be taught to play with their owners. The cat's greatest game, it appears, is to play a little game of hide-and-seek in their litter box.

In conclusion, the value of a pet is directly related to its ability to continually learn and interact with its owner. Thus, since no pet is perfect, we see that an intelligent pet truly makes the best pet. For these reasons, I urge the judges to vote affirmative at the end of today's debate round. Thank you.

Glossary

Term	Definition
Advantage(s)	A positive outcome, typically reversing a HARM, resulting from the affirmative PLAN.
Affirmative	The team or speaker whose job is to support the RESOLUTION.
Agency	The branch of government or department that will pass your plan.
Burden of Proof	The affirmative's obligation to substantiate claims, where the negative may simply cast doubt.
Constructive	A longer speech that sets the parameters for the debate, building arguments and reinforcing them against the other side's attacks.
Contention(s)	A specific reason or logical proof that your side of the RESOLUTION meets the CRITERION for upholding the VALUE.
Criterion / Criteria	The standard(s) used to measure whether or not a VALUE has been met.
Cross-Examination	A short, formal question-and-answer session after each CONSTRUCTIVE speech designed to clarify arguments and expose weaknesses.
Debate	A formal conflict, written or spoken, between competing ideas.
Definition(s)	The meaning of key terms in the RESOLUTION, proposed by the affirmative to set the boundaries of the debate.
Disadvantage	A negative outcome or consequence resulting from the affirmative PLAN.
Enforcement	The people responsible for enforcing your plan.
Ethos	Appeal to ethics.
Evidence	An authority that backs up your argument—includes logical, anecdotal, and empirical information. Team policy debate emphasizes recent empirical evidence while Lincoln-Douglas debate relies more heavily on logic.
Flow Chart	A notepad used during a debate to trace arguments across each speech. See also FLOWING.
Flowing	A method of taking notes that traces arguments across each speech of a debate. See also FLOW CHART.
Funding	The means you will use to pay for your plan.
Harm(s)	A problem that exists because of the current policy.
Term	Definition
Inherency	Whether or not the affirmative's HARMS are caused by the current policy and thus can be fixed by changing it. See STOCK ISSUE(S).
Lincoln-Douglas Debate	A one-on-one debate aiming to persuade of a moral claim or judgment.

Logos	Appeal to logic.
Mandate(s)	The specific law(s) or policy change(s) your plan is proposing.
Negative	The team or speaker whose job is to oppose the RESOLUTION.
Negative Block	Two back-to-back negative speeches comprising the last constructive speech and the first rebuttal.
Observation	One of the pillars of a formal debate. In TEAM POLICY, see DEFINITION(S), HARM(S), PLAN, and ADVANTAGE(S). In LINCOLN-DOUGLAS, see DEFINITION(S), VALUE, CRITERION, and CONTENTION(S).
Pathos	Appeal to emotions.
Plan	A change in policy designed to fix the HARMS.
Prep Time	Time allotted to each speaker or team for the entire debate, to be parceled out before their speeches.
Rebuttal	A shorter speech that summarizes the arguments made in the CONSTRUCTIVES and argues for the superiority of the speaker's side.
Resolution	The subject of the debate. In LINCOLN-DOUGLAS, it is the moral proposition; in TEAM POLICY it is the policy to be changed.
Significance	Whether or not the affirmative's HARMS or ADVANTAGES are important. See STOCK ISSUE(S).
Solution	Another name for the PLAN.
Solvency	Whether or not the affirmative case will solve the HARMS it has identified. See STOCK ISSUE(S).
Status Quo	The current system or policy that the affirmative wants to change.
Stock Issue(s)	Four major issues that the affirmative must prove and the negative may attack. See SIGNIFICANCE, INHERENCY, TOPICALITY, and SOLVENCY.
Summary	A brief explanation in your own words of how your evidence proves your point.
Tagline	A brief statement naming your point (harm, advantage, contention).
Term	Definition
Team Policy Debate	A two-on-two debate aiming to change public policy.
Topicality	Whether or not the affirmative case stays within the boundaries of the RESOLUTION. See STOCK ISSUE(S).
Value	A moral principle, usually abstract, proposed to govern judgments and decision-making.

We believe students will rise to a CHALLENGE.

Our CHALLENGE program, designed for students twelve years and older, provides the perfect setting for students to expand their command of the classical tools of learning—dialectic and rhetorical skills, in particular. Our curriculum path uses a core of familiar classical material and content; however, the Challenge program's primary goal remains mastery of the timeless tools of the classical model. We identify Challenge "levels" rather than grades because students should enroll in the level they are prepared to study.

Our Philosophy

Our rigorous Challenge program stands out from other classical, Christian programs or co-ops for two reasons: First, in each program, one highly qualified, experienced homeschooling parent-tutor partners with students and their parents as a yearlong mentor in all subjects. Second, we believe students of dialectic and rhetoric need help understanding core subjects, equipping them to discover that all knowledge works together in an indivisible "universe" rather than a disconnected "multiverse."

We believe that no subject is taught in isolation. A subject such as science cannot be truly taught without correlating it to math, philosophy, theology, history, and literature. For example, literature analysis cannot be separated from philosophy, theology, history, economics, or science.

Our Challenge tutors seek to give students more than just knowledge in particular subject areas like history or science. Instead, students learn to see how all knowledge glorifies the Lord while also revealing aspects of His divine nature. In this manner, we train our students to become lifelong learners and lovers of God's creation.

In Challenge, our content, assignments, and discussions help students progress from knowledge to understanding to wisdom. Tutors and parents collaborate in guiding students to become godly leaders and confident adults who echo in celebration of their Creator. This partnership between parent and tutor, and our goal of developing leaders with an educated and integrated Christ-centered worldview, makes Classical Conversations unique among other educational services.

Each Challenge program consists of six strands that focus on a particular skill. The Grammar strand is the study of language (Latin). The Exposition and Composition strand encompasses reading and writing. The Debate strand is the study of argument. The Research strand is the study of the natural world. The Rhetoric strand is the study of expression, and the Logic strand is the study of measurement and shape.

The Community

For fifteen weeks in each semester, students participate in a weekly seminar that is facilitated by a trained Challenge tutor. Specific to each Challenge level, the assignment guide is issued by the tutor to each student and outlines the weekly assignments. Students study six classical subjects, utilizing the skill associated with that strand at home while practicing dialectic and rhetorical skills in the weekly seminars. Tutors help point students to the integration of science, history, math, philosophy, literature, and so on, while referring students to the plumb line of God's Word. The weekly seminars give students additional opportunities to hone skills in exposition, speaking, and debate as well as to explore more advanced topics in research and logic seminars.

The Partnership

Although tutors facilitate the weekly community time and lead class discussions, parents continue to be students' primary teachers. The tutor/parent/student partnership is a valuable relationship that fosters accountability for all.

What are the responsibilities of these partners?

- Tutors facilitate class discussions, maintain communication with parents and students regarding student progress, and partner with parents to hold students accountable for their course work.
- Parents assist their students in the completion of the course work, encourage and guide students in the development of good self- and time-management skills, and adjust elements of course work as family dynamics dictate. Parents also assess student work and assign grades.
- Students complete the weekly course work in the time required and prepare for and participate in class discussions.

Visit ClassicalConversations.com for more information on the Challenge Program.